Negotiating Turbulence

Negotiating Turbulence

Purpose-Based, Values-Driven Leadership

John F. Cosgrove

Deeds Publishing | Athens

Published by Deeds Publishing in Athens, GA
www.deedspublishing.com

Printed in The United States of America

Cover design by Mark Babcock

ISBN 978-1-950794-94-2

Books are available in quantity for promotional or premium use. For information, email info@deedspublishing.com.

First Edition, 2023

10 9 8 7 6 5 4 3 2 1

To my daughters Angela and Katie, who have made my life richer beyond measure. To my great friend Cornelius Gabriel Begley (Neil) who taught me more about leadership than anyone. And to my wife Trish whose selfless devotion to others influences so many. Your humility is a trait of greatness and models behaviors sorely needed from all leaders.

Contents

Prologue

Picture a former boss. One you did not respect and probably did not even like. What was it about this person you did not respect? He was a bully. She intimidated you. She was paranoid. He showed favorites. It is hard to respect a boss who is incompetent or cannot be trusted. Many times, bosses disrespected are characterized as only caring about themselves rather than those they lead. Some characterize those bosses as having no integrity.

Thinking about experiences with these people can be uncomfortable, often recalling memories you would like to forget. Yet there can be lessons in reflecting and listing those things you did not appreciate in those people.

Now picture a boss you respected and maybe even liked. What was it about this person that made you appreciate him? She listened to you, or maybe he made you feel valued. She was honest. He was competent. She would never ask you to do something that she would not be willing to do herself.

Thinking about these bosses brings back fond memories and maybe reminders of how much you felt valued. Now, if you had to use one word to distinguish the less-respected bosses from the more-respected bosses, what would it be? My bet is that many of you would say the difference is between "selfless" for the good bosses and "self-serving" for the bad.

I regularly conduct leadership workshops, and I often begin my sessions by asking these questions. You can see the demeanor of the group shift from frowns and aggressive comments in describing the less-respected bosses to smiles and even laughter when describing the respected bosses. My hope is to set the stage for you to begin thinking critically about others before edging towards the more important work of thinking about yourself.

I continue the discussion by posing a question I have asked myself many times: "If I asked everyone who has ever reported to me to indicate where they would place me, either the boss not respected, or the boss respected, how would they answer?" I am sure some, I hope many, would think of me as the respected, selfless, leader. However, I am also sure there are some who would put me in the other category.

Reflecting on the way others may perceive or have perceived your leadership style is important. It is important for all of us to take stock in where we have been as leaders and followers so we can be among the respected leaders of the future.

Throughout this book I will ask you to take an inward journey, reflecting on when and where you did good work and then reflecting on when and where you did not. What attitudes or actions may have landed you on someone's "not respected" list? How can you avoid those mistakes in the future?

The purpose of this book is to help you become a better leader. Maybe it is leading in your workplace, church, family, or any affiliated group. The goal is that years from now, when those who have followed you and reflect on you as their leader, they will describe you with adjectives consistent with a leader they respected most.

The book is organized into five sections. The first two sections address purpose-based and values-driven leadership, the two dynamics that form the character and culture of a group or organization. The remaining sections build on the first two by extending our discussion on purpose-based and values-driven leadership to three other attributes essential to effective leadership: transformational leadership, effective coaching, and motivating our constituents.

However, the foundation of this message rests with an organization having established a purpose that unifies and a set of values that frames behaviors and decisions. This foundation, in part, includes your personal journey to discovering your individual purpose and your individual values. My purpose is to help people understand their great potential and by doing so they will do the same with others.

My personal values are Christ-centered, respect for the individual, loyalty, integrity, and responsible citizenship. Mentioning my personal beliefs are not meant to influence your personal discovery of purpose and values, the subjects of the first two sections. They are periodically mentioned only to make a point. For example, being Christ-centered is core to my personal beliefs and is pictured in Chapter 6 to exemplify the evolution of beliefs one can experience. Its use is not meant to evangelize.

This book will introduce leadership theories discovered by my own experiences and the experiences of other established leaders and scholars. However, these theories are advanced by stories. The stories are all true, some very personal, involving real people. These stories give relevance to the theories with practical leadership application. For example…

Introduction

Some years ago, I purchased a struggling physical fitness gym. It offered workout classes, had an open weights space, and sold memberships on varying levels. It was well equipped with fitness equipment, had committed personal trainers, and an experienced management team. On the surface it looked great, with regular patrons, prospective new members, and an experienced staff that were not informed of the gym's financial struggles.

Our management team, which included me, the lead trainer, and the shift manager, met early on in the acquisition to set out to improve the situation. In particular, we tried new marketing tactics, such as placing ads in local newspapers, running a billboard on a busy highway, and passing out fliers at community events and in neighborhoods for free first classes and discounted memberships.

We aimed to improve the situation, but the efforts weren't paying off financially, and despite our efforts, we continued to struggle. Then one of the managers asked if the gym could help sponsor the local Susan G. Komen Run for the Cure. This request was not a part of our marketing strategy, it was simply an honest ask from someone who cared about the event's cause: a nationally known effort focused on helping find a cure for breast cancer.

The gym had no money to support anything outside the business, but the draw to support the cause was strong. I, along with several other employees, had been deeply impacted by relatives and friends who lost their lives to this dreadful disease. We were inspired, even though the business couldn't foot the bill. We spread word amongst the staff and gym members, and within a few weeks, from the generosity of people's hearts, we gathered enough money to significantly help sponsor the event.

This single suggestion by a staff member created a ripple effect, inspiring our gym community to continue to contribute to other selfless efforts. We became involved in Silver Sneakers, an effort to include the elderly in fitness programs. Our gym staff began to recognize and celebrate the accomplishments of our mentally-challenged members who, despite their disabilities, committed to workout programs to help them realize their potential. These efforts unified staff and members behind causes bigger than ourselves. We had found our purpose.

Our unified identity transcended product or market life cycles, technological breakthroughs, management fads, individual leaders, and politics. It evolved from simply providing people a place to exercise into something much more: helping others realize their great potential. The gym transformed from a place into a tool, a tool that would help us make members of our community better. It was selfless, or in other words, wholesome. And, maybe by accident, it was good for business.

Our management still paid attention to marketing, balance sheets, membership count, and other important dynamics. However, once we shifted attention to our overarching purpose of helping others understand their great potential, the business became increasingly profitable. Today, the gym still survives many years later and under new ownership. In my view, it was leadership embracing its unifying purpose that saved the business and propelled it towards success.

The core to effective leadership is to unify a group or organization towards a purpose that members individually would consider wholesome and good. The first section of this book will help you discover your true individual purpose. It will help align your individual purpose with the purpose of any business, club, church, or any organization you are associated with. As the group moves toward realizing its purpose, constituents will be moving toward their individual purposes as well. Imagine how motivating that could be and how more effective we could be as leaders just by understanding and appreciating the purpose of those we lead, while helping them understand that by the organization realizing its purpose, they will move toward realizing their individual purpose.

Also core to effective leadership is to have guidelines that frame behaviors and decisions. I call these *individual* and *organizational values*. It is important that individual values be reasonably aligned with the organization's or group's values. Let's take the fitness facility. As a group we spent time exploring our personal values. From that collaboration we established a set of organizational values that framed the business's decisions and behaviors. One of the values was "Respect for the Individual." Embedded in the definition of this value is a sense of respecting differences and appreciating the special gifts unique to each individual.

The fitness facility had a manager who had problems working with women. That concerned me. I was getting complaints from both staff and members. The first was a female staff member complaining about unwanted advances. Another staff manager, again female, complained about inappropriate language with a sexual flavor. Another member complained about inappropriate comments as women were exercising. These incidents happened over a period of several months.

He had some qualities I appreciated. He was involved in our philanthropic efforts and, in fact, focused on helping senior citizens have easier access to the gym. He appeared to be engaged with the members in a very healthy way, providing them encouragement. He actively participated in our weekly meetings that always highlighted at least one of our values by discussing how that value engaged a decision or behavior in a positive way. We often discussed our value of *Respect for the Individual.*

At first, I thought his inappropriate interactions with women resulted from poor judgment, and so I tried using coaching to adjust his behavior. After each incident, he and I had candid conversations that specifically addressed these complaints and how these incidents concerned me about his alignment with the value of "Respect for the Individual," particularly when it came to women. However, the evidence continued to mount, and it became apparent that his failings with women were less about his judgment and more about his value of respecting others not being aligned with both my values and the organization's. His behavior reflected *his* values, and values seldom change quickly.

To keep him as an employee would have signaled to everyone associated with this business that his behavior honored our value of *Respect for the Individual.* It did not. He was let go. *Values are guiding principles and tenets that frame our decisions and behaviors.* They can remind us to get back on track when we get off course. Good coaching could have brought him back on course, if his behavior was more a matter of judgment. It was not poor judgment; it was misaligned individual values.

When I reflect on the values of the leaders I respected versus the leaders I did not respect, I conclude that the leaders I did not respect had not spent time reflecting on personal values and did not care what my values were. I would guess our values would be quite different. Hence, I was frustrated. With the leaders I did respect, I could clearly identify their personal values, was certain that they had an appreciation for my personal values, and that our values were reasonably aligned.

The second section of this book will help you discover, or confirm, your individual values. It is important that leaders clearly know their own values and the values of those they lead. This, coupled with understanding the values of the organization, forms a basis for decision making and behaviors that are acceptable or are not. *Aligned values coupled with complimenting individual and group purpose forms the culture of an organization.*

The remaining sections of this book will help you develop habits and processes for embedding purpose-based and values-driven leadership into the fabric of an organization. Transformational leadership development, coaching that is values driven and purpose based, while motivating constituents, are all important to good leadership and are included in these remaining sections.

The stories presented in this book are true. Many are very personal and reflect my own experiences and decisions. Some of these decisions, in retrospect, were quite good and probably would have landed me on the most respected list, while other decisions could have been better and would probably have landed me on the "other" list. I leave nothing out. My intent is to give relevancy to the point. My hope is these stories encourage you to discover your values or confirm the values you have already discovered while, at the same time, frame or confirm your purpose that will define you as a respected leader.

I wrote this book because it is sorely needed. We have experienced poor leadership that is self-serving and just plain embarrassing in every sector of society. I would contend that much of this flawed leadership is attributed to an environment void of values and/or working towards a purpose we can be proud of collectively. My greatest hope is that my children, grandchildren, and their children, along with anyone else reading this book, realize their great leadership potential and with this realization understand their great value to our community.

Each section will include Action Steps. These action steps suggest a proven process to implement the ideas of the section. In addition, each section lists *Contributing Works*. This work lists other books and articles relevant to the subject. These lists may help the reader look at what I present from a different angle or perspective. Some work that is listed helped inspire thought and reflection as to the relevancy of my personal leadership story. I found it important to recognize some of these fine authors and allow the reader the option to also read related works. My prayer is that through this effort we will all experience better leadership in our communities.

Section I

The Destination: Purpose

Group Culture: $f(\textbf{purpose}, \text{values})$

The ideology, or a culture, of any organization is a function of **a unifying purpose** and a set of values that frame decisions and behaviors.

I am a private pilot and have spent many hours in the cockpit of small four seat airplanes flying according to a submitted flight plan. Every flight plan has three main parts: a start point, a route, and a destination. Any experienced pilot can tell you that no matter how well thought out a flight plan, it will never be followed exactly. Once airborne, wind may blow you left or right of your planned route; you may maneuver around dark clouds; air traffic control may vector you to a different route not in the plan; unexpected turbulence is a certainty and will require you to compensate; or a storm may force you to land, allowing it to pass.

Despite those changes, you constantly try to move the airplane in the direction of your destination. Your instruments help you follow your route and, when turbulence and storms are encountered, your instruments keep you pointed towards the destination.

Without your instruments, you could be suspended in a massive space not knowing where you are, what direction you are headed, or whether there might be engine performance problems. Just as pilots need their instruments to get to their destination, leaders need values to achieve their purpose. Leading without a focused purpose and void of values is no different than a pilot trying to negotiate turbulence with no destination and no instruments, suspended in space. Crashing is inevitable. Let's take an example.

For years, Wells Fargo had a reputation for sound management. Its reputation was founded on its vision to "satisfy our customers' needs and help them succeed financially." Currently, on the company's web site, it states:

> Our vision has nothing to do with transactions, pushing products, or getting bigger for the sake of bigness. It's about building **lifelong relationships,** one customer at a time…We strive to be recognized by our stakeholders as setting the standard among the world's great companies for **integrity** and **principled performance.** This is more than just doing the right thing. We also have to do it in **the right way.**

In 2016, Wells Fargo was fined $185 million from the Consumer Financial Protection Bureau, the Office of the Comptroller of the Currency, and the City and County of Los Angeles for the creation of 1.5 million fake deposit accounts and more than 500,000 fake credit cards, all in customers' names and without their permission. In 2017, it was discovered that a more accurate number was 3.5 million fake accounts. As the investigation continued, it became clear that this was not simply the mistakes of a few employees. Rather, it was indicative of a corrupt culture.

It was even discovered that a former wealth manager had tried to report suspected fraud on the hotline. Rather than investigating his claims, he was fired. Efforts were being made to cover up the truth. This former manager would eventually win a lawsuit against Wells Fargo and be awarded $5.4 million in damages.

Other lawsuits ensued, ranging from issues with overcharging small business retailers to problems with community lending and discrimination. Unfortunately, it appears the pressure to win contests and receive recognition contributed to behavior far removed from what was stated on their website. Self-serving motives (remember the least respected leader) took the place of the more selfless motives of serving the client. It seemed that integrity, one of the written values of the organization, did not apply, or was forgotten.

I use this example not to knock business goals or internal contests. On the contrary, I believe that it is important for any business to have short term goals, to set achievement standards and to encourage healthy competition. However, if these goals are achieved at the expense of violating the values that are supposed to guide our decisions and behaviors, we can lose sight of the purpose that is supposed to unite everyone's efforts.

Like Wells Fargo, too many leadership cultures seem to have a higher priority of taking care of self, versus taking care of those they lead and serve. Self-serving purpose can overshadow the selfless purpose intended to unite everyone. Values are rationalized away so that the instruments needed to keep us on course towards a great destination no longer exist.

For the politician, this may mean it is more important to be reelected than to serve the public. For the business leader, it may mean it is more important to protect a position or increase wealth rather than helping others attain promotions or get paid fairly. The overarching wholesome purpose practiced by the servant leader is replaced by a private self-serving purpose, and thus, there is no clarity that unifies efforts towards the destination. Similarly, the path toward that destination is clouded because of the absence of values that guide behaviors and decisions.

In reading this book, you will be inspired to self-reflect and discover, or rediscover, your personal purpose. You will discover, or confirm, your own values and evaluate how your values are aligned with your group's values. I hope they are reasonably aligned. If they are not, I hope you transition to a place where your individual values are aligned with the values of the organization you represent.

Before we get going, it is important to understand that good leadership starts with good theory. Good theory will tell us what will happen before we experience it. Good theory can help define good strategy, tactics, decision making, strategic plans, and so on. It justifies a course of action. Experience and relevant information are wonderful teachers and can be important when making critical decisions. However, the pain of gaining experience may not be worth its cost. We do not have to go through multiple marriages to be good spouses, nor are we willing to sacrifice our first born on the table of learning so we can master parenting the last child.

It is similar when it comes to hiring people to lead our organizations. Is it worth making critical hiring mistakes until we finally get it right? I think not. Therefore, theory is important.

This isn't to say experience doesn't matter. It does. Good leaders often make decisions based on what has happened in their lives and in the lives of others. Part of learning and creating a learning environment in your organization involves reflections on happenings—the good, and bad, based on the results rendered. We should learn all we can from experience, from scholars, from mentors, and the like.

However, this does not solve the fundamental problem of what information and advice you should accept or what past experience is relevant for future decisions. I suggest applying good theory to information and advice in making decisions. My theories represent a partnership of work between the scholarly community, the practical leader, and my own endeavors.

Section One and Section Two form the foundation for the remaining sections. It starts with the theory that the culture of an organization is a function of how well the team understands and strives towards realizing a purpose while abiding by a set of group or organizational values.

Culture: f(purpose, values)

A purpose is the principal unifying force towards defining success. However, that success is not at all cost. This is where values come in. Values are the rules that frame decisions and behaviors. When organizations fail, like Wells Fargo, it is usually because they lose sight of their purpose in favor of more short-sighted objectives, or they drift away from making decisions and behaving based on a set of guiding principles called values.

Some notable scholars claim that purpose and values form the ideology of an organization. Put another way, purpose and values form the manner in which individuals of the group think, work together, motivate, coach, communicate, and transform. Though it is the basis for everything, the leader, like the pilot, needs training on how to use the instruments. Similarly, leaders need values training, and that topic forms the second section of this book. However, efforts are meaningless unless we have a destination, or purpose. So, that is where we start.

1. Shooting at the Wrong Target

Matthew Emmon's primary vocation is as a Certified Public Accountant. Uniquely, his secondary vocation was that of a sharpshooter. In fact, in 2004, he had a reputation for being the best sharpshooter in the world, and expectedly competed in the Olympic Games in Athens, Greece. However, a series of very unusual events were about to take place. For one thing, his rifle was mysteriously sabotaged in the run-up to the Games. When he took it out of his locker at the US training center, it just felt wrong, and sure enough, a brief inspection showed that it had been tampered with and was no longer working properly.

Emmons, who was the reigning world champion in the 50-meter rifle three positions, was forced to borrow a weapon from his former university teammate Amber Darlaand. It proved to be a blessing. He prospered with his new rifle, winning the gold medal in the small-bore prone position by a margin of just over one point from Germany's Christian Lusch. Two days later, he had the chance to make history when he lined up for the finals of the three positions competition. Up until now, nobody had ever won both events at the same Games.

Due to his commanding lead at the end of the competition, all he needed for his second gold medal was to hit the target. By his own account, he lined up on Lane 3 and began his steady breathing ritual to calm himself, then he squeezed the trigger. The bullet hit dead center bullseye at his intended target. The problem was that Emmons aimed at the target in lane 2, not lane 3. Red flags from officials were raised, and Emmons' dropped from first to eighth in the standings. An unknown Chinese sharpshooter named Jia Zhanbo won the gold medal. Later Emmons would say that before this event he had always lined up the correct lane with the appropriate target, but this time he did not. In the aftermath, he was just focused on calming himself down.

This story resonates with me on several levels. First, it prompts me to ask myself: What target am I aiming at, and is it the right target? I am talking about my life's "target." What is my target or purpose? Is the purpose worth a lifelong effort to realize? Second, as I go through life, growing and maturing, how have I been distracted from realizing my purpose in favor of other short-term priorities? How often do I check my lane to make sure my target (or purpose) is the right one? These are "life" questions.

Now I ask you: What target are you aiming at? Are you even aiming at a target at all, or are you just reacting to life without regard for purpose? How can we be on course without knowing where we want the course to take us? How can we focus toward a common objective when the common objective is splintered by the uncommon or the unaligned vision of individual team members?

When I was in high school, my boyhood dream was to be an NBA basketball player. At West Point, my goal was to simply graduate. When I graduated, my goal was to be a successful Army officer, maybe command a battalion, or brigade, perhaps become a general. When I decided to leave the Army to become a business-man, my goal became to succeed in position and to make money, to become a corporate vice-president, president, director, or CEO.

As I achieved these goals, upon reflection, I realized these goals were being confused with purpose. They were good goals and im-portant to have and achieve, but they were not my life's purpose. I was shooting at the wrong target. Goals that were about myself, my own position or accomplishment or wealth, may be worth-while, but they fell short of establishing a life's purpose that gave me a reason for having goals at all. Furthermore, a life's purpose that is wholesome and good and durable would be less about my-self and what I could do for me, and more about what I can do for others.

2. Days Gone By

Seldom does a week pass that I do not glance at the picture below of my West Point classmates that sits on my bookshelf. It was taken just a few weeks before our graduation. These were and are my very best friends. It has been over forty-five years since we graduated, and collectively these are still the finest people I know.

West Point Classmates

This picture was taken in 1975 when we were around 22 years old and reminds me of days gone by. Each of us had goals and dreams of what we wanted to become. I am the dark-haired guy standing about in the middle with my left palm and hand raised up resting on the staircase wall. I was going to be a successful Airborne Ranger Infantry officer and maybe even become a general. Little did I know I would leave the service after twelve years and pursue a career in the financial industry.

Much happened throughout my life that I could not have anticipated, and my destination, or purpose, changed. My course obviously changed as well. The same was true for many of my classmates. Towards the bottom left is Scott. He has the "A" on his jacket indicating success as an intercollegiate athlete. He was a great swimmer, certainly, one of the best athletes in the group. He had conditioned himself so much he decided he had enough of "working out." He would marry, have children, and embark on a successful business career after leaving the Army five years later. But before that business career would ever get established, he died due to poor health choices.

Standing in front of the group is Bob. You can see his eventual baldness begin to set in. He would later have the courage to overcome alcoholism, marry a wonderful California woman, and retire as a very successful businessman in the computer industry. I also see John. He is the first one sitting on the staircase wall. I attended his wedding. That marriage ended in divorce. No wonder—he had met the love of his life the same year this photo was taken and just did not know it. Years later, and with some pain I am sure, he finally married that love of his life. He currently is an active pilot and works as a director of a mission critical technology, cyber, and information technology firm.

Just to John's right is Chuck. Only his head and face are showing. He stayed in the service for years and toward the end of his military career was stationed in Rwanda. On April 6, 1994, the Rwanda president along with members of his cabinet were murdered. What ensued was an estimated 800,000 men, women, and children slaughtered, many with machetes. My friend Chuck arrived in Rwanda as a military liaison just days prior to the death of the president and the beginning of the bloodshed. It is reported he saved many lives and saw things I can only imagine. He is a true hero. He returned inflicted with PTSD and, with help, emerged from that challenge a success.

And the list goes on; professional officers, an adjutant general, a professional raft guide, English professors, high school teachers, a pastor, business owners, physicians, CEOs, successful and, as you would expect, some unsuccessful husbands and fathers. For the most part, I would guess, few of us ended up where we thought we would. We didn't start our path after graduation with the intent of getting divorced, becoming an alcoholic, dying after a sudden health decline, or exposing ourselves to genocide. But these things happened.

At 22, I suspect you may have been like me and didn't spend much time thinking about a life purpose. Maybe, like me, you allowed someone else to do that thinking for you. I allowed the Army or corporate America to do that thinking. Maybe your life took unexpected turns in ways you could not have predicted. Maybe those turns contributed to your maturity. As I matured, I became better at allocating my time, talent, and energies towards things more meaningful. My life's purpose began to form.

By virtue of your reading this book maybe you are searching for purpose or the realization of an already-discovered purpose. Looking back, I think my effectiveness as a leader improved as I developed, and committed to, a purpose that was less about me and more about others. Today my life's purpose is to help others understand their great potential.

I firmly believe that if you take the time to figure out your life's purpose, you will look back on it as one of your most important discoveries, not only as a leader but as a person. During the times of turbulence, when things are confusing and difficult, you, the leader, will remind your followers of your purpose, their purpose, and you will be pointing your team in a direction that is clear, and you will be followed.

3. Personal Purpose

Pointed in the Right Direction

*Note reference at the end of this section

To discover your personal purpose, we need to reflect on what is most important to you as an individual. From this reflection can grow a meaningful purpose statement that can help keep you pointed in the right direction. We will extend this to discover how your personal life's purpose can, at least in part, be fulfilled by focusing on the purpose of any group you are affiliated with, but particularly your workplace. Identifying with a group's purpose is critical to developing goals, strategic plans, coaching, motivating, and transforming, which is dealt with in Sections 3, 4, and 5.

I believe that much trouble often is associated with an over emphasis on shorter term goals that are often confused with a life's purpose. Examples for me were goals of becoming an NBA basketball player, a military general, or a rich businessman. Short term goals may mean allocating too much time and energy towards selling more than anyone else, promotions, bonuses, winning basket-ball games, or organizational awards and recognition. It is natural to work towards such goals for they are concrete and measurable. These goals are good if they do not receive more attention than they deserve (as was the case with Wells Fargo). They contrast with the more intangible focuses of spending time with your children and spouse or efforts to selflessly coach.

A wholesome purpose transforms the typical goals of wealth and promotion to something deeper and more real. I would de-scribe "wholesome" as selfless action that focuses on a greater good. It is probably consistent with how you would describe the "re-spected" leader earlier. A wholesome purpose subordinates small distractions and irrelevant activities by unifying the group towards more meaningful activity. For Example...

Wine Over Water

Some years ago, I worked for a large nationally known brokerage firm and was responsible for running a region in the central part of the United States. I recall being a focused leader driven by the objectives of my firm—objectives that changed annually. My per-sonal purpose was whatever the firm told me it was, and it seemed my bonuses depended on how successful I was in accomplishing those objectives. At the same time, I was a dedicated father of two wonderful daughters who were, and are today, lights of my life. If you would have asked me then, "What is your purpose?" I would have said being a father, a husband, and striving for executive ex-cellence. Excellence meant accomplishing those annual corporate objectives.

One day the mayor of our community came to me and asked

me to sponsor a major downtown event called "Wine Over Water." Tickets would be sold with all proceeds going towards the development of the downtown. In exchange, my operation was promised great local recognition. I was able to invite my financial advisors and their selected clients to an exclusive reception. It turned out to be a great event and, when it was over, everyone thought I was wonderful for supporting the downtown development. Most importantly, this event would surely help me accomplish that year's corporate objectives.

Sponsoring this event contributed to my organization's success. My financial advisors were able to deepen their relationships with their best clients while having the opportunity to develop new clients. The firm, in general, was viewed by the community as "giving back" in a way that was good and right. Looking back, however, I see the event as a missed opportunity. Even to this day, I have no idea if our efforts actually did anything to revive the downtown. You see, my purpose was not to help the downtown or be philanthropic at all, my purpose was to accomplish the objectives of my firm, such as generating revenue, developing new clients, making money, and other dictated objectives.

The opportunity to rally other business leaders and encourage their involvement? Missed. The opportunity to include the downtown nonprofit community like the YMCA or the Boys and Girls Clubs? Missed. The opportunity to partner with the Chamber of Commerce? Also missed. And the list goes on. If I applied a purpose that included improving the community that we live and work in, maybe we would have generated even more recognition for ourselves simply by putting ourselves second and others first. If I had put our community first, we may have been able to improve the lives of so many. However, I was so focused on the short-term corporate objectives that I failed to recognize a purpose within myself that had vision, could be extended well into the future, and could be used to define my reason for being. I needed a purpose that was less about me and more about others, including those I led.

4. Commit to a Purpose

Individual purpose extends beyond job, family, economic, and community efforts. An individual's purpose does not include *some* of these things; it includes *all* these things. It should be applied to all parts of our life and it seldom, if ever, changes. It is the reason for how we think and how we act. It brings clarity to a complex existence and keeps us pointed in a direction that is unique and special to each individual. It justifies the 'why' we do or do not do some things. Without a purpose we can't have a destination.

A personal purpose can provide daily discipline that informs the actions we choose to take — or not take. It is a principal ingredient directly related to how we live. If your personal life purpose is to be a successful executive, father, and husband (which is fine) what happens when these purposes are in conflict? If your personal life's purpose is to make a million dollars, be an NBA basketball player, become a doctor, or buy a home, what happens when these purposes are achieved, or not? Does your life begin, or end, based on a particular outcome? Who benefits if you realize your purpose? When your purpose is short-sighted, it is usually driven by economics or ego. *No one benefits but you.* A purpose like that is selfish and inconsistent with the concepts of service. It probably describes the purpose of the leader you did not respect.

I am hoping you can appreciate the difference between having a purpose that is significant and selfless, and a purpose that changes frequently, is short-sighted, and is usually self-serving in nature. We need selfless leaders with one big purpose that is personal and expressed authentically. Throughout the ensuing chapters of this book, I invite you to come with me to discover your purpose—your destination.

Discovering Your Purpose—It is Halftime

Bob Buford, in his 1994 book, *Halftime,* presents a process for developing a personal purpose and how to construct a plan for its realization. Buford describes his readers as having some life experience and being engaged in a life-long athletic contest where they have completed the first half and are now headed for the locker room to discuss a plan for final victory. Maybe during the first half of life they rushed through college, fell in love, married, and embarked on a career aspiring to achieve some success. They acquired a few things to make the journey comfortable. They have been scared, happy, and sad. They have been challenged and have met challenges with success and with failure. They have learned from their experiences so that at halftime they can develop a strategy that will lead to victory, or rather, realize a wholesome life's purpose that is significant.

My first half put importance on acquiring things that would indicate I was successful to others. I do not apologize for my emphasis on success. It was a part of me then and is a part of me now. Graduating from West Point and having a successful military career that included being selected for promotions and sensitive positions was important. Succeeding in my corporate life which included competing for recognition and receiving financial reward was important.

However, during my halftime I discovered that while these things *were* important, they were just not *as* important as I thought. To use Buford's theory, I transitioned by applying less emphasis to what was *important* and more emphasis to what was *significant*. *What was significant would inform my legacy which was more about the positive impact I could have on others and less on myself.*

The transition from the first half to the second half is different for each individual. It can happen when you least expect it. Maybe it is during a vocational transition or maybe the death of a loved one. Or maybe it was during a time when you just knew a change had to take place. Buford's experience in halftime was similar to mine. He experienced the unexpected death of his son, coupled with a vocational transition. I experienced the unexpected death of my wife, also followed by a vocational transition.

My halftime lasted several years. It was difficult, but the half-time journey can lead to discovering your purpose and that is critical to becoming an effective leader. In fact, it can change your life.

Discovering this purpose demands an inward journey. What is important? What do you believe? What is core? What are your great successes, and why are they successes? What are your greatest failures and why are they failures? What did you learn from these successes and failures? What makes you angry, and what makes you passionate? What do you want your legacy to be? I begin many of my leadership workshops by asking participants to list the five most important things in their lives in order of importance. This is the first step in discovering your purpose. Some of the most common responses are:

Family	Christ
Health	Boat
Home	Kids
Job	Grandchildren
Money	Nephews/Nieces
Smiles	Coworkers
Laughter	Church
Pets	Mom/Dad
Faith	Fitness
Wellness	Health
Legacy	Extended Family
Togetherness	Boat
Fishing	Competition
Hunting	Travel
	Self-growth
Learning	Fun
Vacation Time	Security

Listing the first three most important things is usually easy. Maybe it is a husband or wife, children, or grandchildren. Sometimes it is a religious or Christian expression of faith, like following Jesus or building a relationship with God, or maybe an overall commitment to a more general concept such as spirituality.

The last two or three most important things may take some further pondering. Maybe health, job, or vocation, hunting or fishing, extended family, friends, or even a pet. Give it a try and see what you come up with. You may better understand your current list by reflecting on how these important things changed during different stages of your life.

For example, for me there was a time when basketball, my mother, high school grades, or my boss having a favorable view of me were very important. As I grew older and had a family, transitioned careers, and experienced some life hardships, my list changed. Winning basketball games or impressing my boss were replaced by being Christ-centered, being an effective leader in my church and community, or being a trusted friend.

Buford suggests you place your answers in categories and, symbolically, place those categories "in a box." I went through this drill several years ago and decided my important things could fall into three categories: family (wife, children, grandchildren, and extended family), Christ (a personal relationship with Jesus), and health. Taking my role as it pertained to each category, I asked myself three times, building on each previous answer, "Why is this important?" As an example, here is what I discovered about myself.

Family

What is important about being a husband, father, and grandfather?

Because this is a family leadership role, and I can have positive impact on the people I love and care about the most.

Why is it important to positively impact these people you love?

Because in that role their happiness and satisfaction in life may be enhanced.

Why is that important?

Because if they are happy and satisfied with their lives, perhaps they can realize their own great potential and be positive influencers in their communities.

Christ

What is important about a relationship with Jesus Christ?
Because I want to go to heaven.
To get to heaven, *what is important?*
For me to go to heaven I must serve Jesus.
And *what is important* to serving Jesus?
To serve Jesus I must help fulfill his great commission of making disciples and help others understand their great potential in serving Christ.

Health

Why is it important to be healthy?
Because part of having a happy and fulfilled life is feeling well.

What is important about having a happy and fulfilled life?
To feel good about myself.

What is important about feeling good about you?
If I feel good about myself, I am better equipped to realize my great potential in serving my family, friends, and community.

* * *

The following purpose statement evolved out of this process:

John Cosgrove's Purpose Statement

My purpose is to help others understand their great potential and by doing so maybe they will do the same for others in their community.

It is my rallying cry and what I try to achieve as a leader and person. Try it for yourself and see what you discover:

1. List the five most important things.
2. Categorize them into boxes.
3. Ask, "Why is this important?" Repeat the questioning at least two more times to your answer.
4. Discover a common theme and frame your purpose statement.

* * *

To review, Buford encourages people to put what is important into categories. For Buford, the three categories were family, religious beliefs, and career. For me it is family, my relationship with Jesus, and health. He encourages a discussion involving your spouse or significant other and two trusted friends before proclaiming the one thing that will define your reason for being or life's purpose.

Go to each category and ask yourself "Why is this important?" Keep asking it until the answer for all three categories is the same or similar. That is your purpose. My 'second half' of life is not about collecting things but providing things to others, that learning never stops, and that my life is no longer controlled by the goals and objectives of those around me (though important) but rather controlled by a purpose that is significant. The first half was about doing important things, while the second half is about doing things of significance.

5. Discovering Their Purpose

The Brick Layers

*Note reference at the end of this section

Visualize every member of your team having their own list of what is important to them and having their own individual purpose statement.

Not only is it important to be intentional about what is most important; it is also important to share what is important to you with those you hold dear, along with coworkers, or anyone where a relationship exists. This sharing may help you understand and appreciate each other more. In his 1999 article *Managing One's Self,* Peter Drucker argues that the concept of organizations built on trust does not mean everyone necessarily likes each other, but it does mean that everyone understands one another. Understanding starts with knowing what is important to one another. This extends into knowing each other's purpose and each other's core values.

Let's consider three bricklayers building a wall. You ask the first bricklayer, "What are you doing?" He replies, "Building a wall." You go to the second bricklayer and ask, "What are you doing?" He replies, "Building a church." You approach the third bricklayer and ask again, "What are you doing?" He responds, "Building the house of God." All three are doing the same thing for very different reasons. The first brick layer is building the wall probably to earn money to support his family. The second brick layer also needs to earn a living but in building this wall there is meaning in knowing that he is doing something bigger than himself; he is building a church. The third brick layer is also earning a living to provide for his family but, unlike the second brick layer, is building more than a church, rather, he is building the actual house of God.

If you were a spiritual leader in this church, it seems like this would be important information to know. The leadership implications are the leader's understanding as to what really drives each individual. But sometimes there is more to understanding purpose. For example, let's look at the sidewalk sweeper and the story of Marge.

Helping Realize Purpose—The Sidewalk Sweeper and The Story of Marge

I was giving a speech titled "Purpose-Based, Values-Driven Leadership" to the staff of a local college. Towards the front of the auditorium, which seated about four hundred people, sat a man in overalls. I asked him what he did at the university. He said he swept the sidewalks. In front of a capacity crowd, we began a personal conversation.

"Why is that important?" I asked.

"Because I think it is important for the students to walk on clean sidewalks," he answered.

"Why is it important for the students to walk on clean sidewalks?"

"If the students walk on clean sidewalks, they will respect their school more."

He was beginning to get irritated. He did not expect a line of questions in front of roughly four hundred staff members, including the university president. I pressed on. "Why is it important for the students to walk on clean walks and respect their school?"

"If the students respect their school, they will learn to respect their communities they live in and become better citizens."

"So, your purpose is to help the students develop themselves to becoming good citizens in their communities."

"I guess you are right."

He was smiling. So, as you fill in your boxes described in Chapter 4 ask yourself three times "Why is this important?" If you really think about it, you will come up with a life purpose. Maybe you will lead others to discovering their purpose.

Years after the "Wine Over Water" missed opportunity, I took over a similar position with another large financial firm. I headquartered this operation out of Orlando, Florida. I was told prior to taking the position that the Chief Operations Officer (we will call her Marge) had been struggling and probably should be replaced. This was a problem I would have to deal with. Within several weeks it became clear Marge had a credibility problem. People seemed to like her well enough; they just did not consider her competent or credible.

To my surprise, I discovered Marge was not registered as a financial principal. Being a financial principal requires additional training and the passing of a very comprehensive examination. Though difficult, it is a basic requirement for assuming a management position in the financial industry. She had made efforts to be registered, but each effort ended with her failing the examination, preventing her from being able to legally administer many basic operational requirements. This impacted the workload of those around her, including me. Marge also had a reputation of being sporadically late and, upon occasion, would have unpredictable absences.

When I invited the management team to share the most important things in their lives, Marge listed her nephew as number one, her cat was second, and her job was third. It turned out her nephew had a history of behaviors that would unexpectedly cause her to miss work or be late. Her cat was old and needed care at unexpected times. Only a few close friends knew of these challenges. We now understood. People she had worked with for years did not know how important her nephew and cat were to her. Her job was listed as number three in terms of importance, which is a high priority, but not as high as her nephews or her cat.

Like many of us, Marge had never given serious thought to an individual life's purpose. Through our discussion she discovered that she had a passion for helping the disenfranchised—like a challenged nephew or an aging cat. I was sure her purpose existed somewhere in that space. I had developed my purpose by now, which is to help others understand their great potential, and that now included Marge. Marge's purpose evolved into helping those who could not help themselves. I appreciated that purpose. I believed Marge's coworkers would be willing to be patient with her a little longer now that they had a better understanding of her situation.

However, if Marge was to gain credibility, she had to become more competent, which included becoming a registered financial principal. At my insistence, she started studying again and, again, failed the exam. At the same time, I had to take a commodity registration exam. I needed a 70% grade to pass but received a 69% score. I announced I was going to retake the exam in thirty days (the minimum time to retake the exam). Marge was inspired to do the same. She did, and she finally passed (and so did I). Getting that registration not only allowed her to take the responsibility required of her position, but she also gained the knowledge and confidence that helped her gain credibility. Marge went on to get promoted and eventually retire with great dignity and respect.

The decision to work with Marge in helping her understand her great potential not only benefited her, but the company as well. In taking a more coercive approach, like firing her, as I was advised to do, I would have had to replace her. Not an easy task. Marge herself would have to recover emotionally and financially from losing her job. Marge's nephew, and probably even her cat, would have felt the effects of the job loss. Because my actions were driven by my purpose, to help others understand their great potential (my rallying cry), the company and Marge experienced a better outcome.

The key to helping Marge find success was in having her colleagues, including myself, understand what was important to her and to inspire her to discover her purpose that transcended her job and family challenges. People, myself included, became more patient when we understood the importance she placed on helping the disenfranchised (Marge's rallying cry) while also making an effort to be more competent. This was not easy for Marge, or me either.

Inspiring followers to make changes, take risks, and trust a new message that is less about short term success and more about purpose is hard and takes courage. There were times, I am sure, when Marge probably wished I would just stop and go away. If I would have given up on my plan for Marge's development and chosen an easier course, I would have given up on Marge and, in turn, failed in my effort to realize my purpose. I could not do that. *Good leaders inspire others to believe in them, but great leaders inspire others to believe in themselves.* That inspiration is captured by understanding what is important to each other; knowing what is important to each member of the team, along with understanding each member's purpose (and values, the subject of the next section). That understanding can truly unify an organization.

6. Aligning Our Purpose

The Business Practices of the Trappist Monks

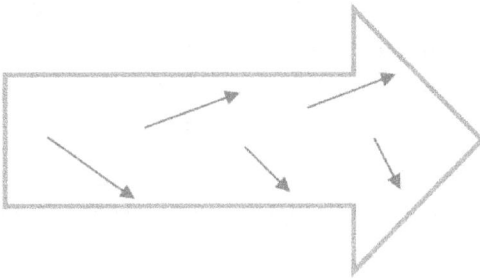

Note reference at the end of this section

Organizations with a unifying purpose have leaders that align individual purposes with the organization's purpose thereby as the individual realizes their purpose so does the organization.

"For 1,500 years monasteries all over the world have been calling men and women to a life of prayer and work according to the rule of St. Benedict." Thus, begins the book written by August Turak, titled *The Business Practices of the Turkish Monks*. Just outside

Charleston, South Carolina exists more than three thousand acres that make up the Our Lady of Mepkin Abbey. It is here that Turak lived with the Trappist Monks for three years. His experience is captured in his book.

The monks were known for having a very successful egg business. Throughout South Carolina, vendors would travel to buy their wonderful eggs. Grocery stores throughout the region would purchase the monks' eggs at a premium price. The chickens were cared for solely by the monks and the occasional guest, like Turak. Revenue from the business easily supported the monastery. Turak wanted to discover the secrets to their business success. And discover he did!

One morning, to the surprise of everyone, a group of protestors were picketing outside of the monastery, protesting cruelty to chickens. Apparently, this was a national movement, and the notoriety of the monks' business made them a target. The monks' solution to the unrest was simple: they got out of the egg business. They sold all their chickens and never sold another egg. Instead, they shifted into fertilizer and mushroom enterprises. Before long, this business was more successful than the egg business. Turak discovered the secret. Yes, the monks worked hard and had some basic business practices, but the secret was that they had no secret at all. Turak writes:

> Paradoxically, the reasons for the Mepkin's business success are that the monks are not actually in business at all. Instead, they are utterly committed to a high overarching mission and management philosophy this book will refer to as service and selflessness. Business success for the monks is merely the by-product of a life well lived.

The monks have an overarching vision that rallies the entire monastery to a common calling of service and selflessness: serving their community. With service and selflessness, they model behaviors that have extended their practice into a very successful business model. Instead of thinking about their purpose only occasionally, they think about their purpose all the time. Their purpose is lived every day and genuinely drives the decision making that determines every activity, big or small. This means each individual's purpose is reasonably aligned with the group. Turak describes the monks as if they were great archers shooting over all the chaos and distractions, aiming at their overarching purpose.

Their business practices are merely a byproduct of realizing their purpose of living a life of selfless service. Self-serving behaviors and decisions along with over emphasis on short term organizational goals not related to the purpose are easily recognized and often become extinct.

This alignment of individual purpose to group purpose is critical. You cannot make someone adopt a purpose. Like the monks who are drawn to their work because of aligned purpose with the monastery, it is important that individual members of your organization have individual purposes that are reasonably aligned with the organization's purpose. As the organization realizes its purpose, so does each member, to varying degrees, realize their individual purpose. Jim Collins, in his 1996 article titled "Building Your Company's Vision" terms this as *core ideology*, or, what we stand for and why we exist. Core ideology inspires unity, not differentiation. It attracts people of like purpose and values. It is something that individuals need not be convinced of, rather, they are already convinced.

7. A Rallying Cry

Followers want to know what their leaders believe and stand for. They want this belief to inspire a rallying cry that is meaningful, significant, and serves as an example of how they may be able to realize *their* personal purpose. Leaders inspire people to unite behind a common cause. It can be a word, phrase, or event that captures and helps people understand their own reason for being.

Who can forget "Remember the Alamo"? That rallying cry, inspired by the massacre of Colonel Travis and his men at the Alamo during the Texas Revolution, would later spur on the forces of Sam Houston at San Jacinto. Patrick Henry's "Give me liberty or give me death" speech inspired a nation's purpose to fight for freedom, while the Declaration of Independence continues to rally that same nation to stay on freedom's course. To include others in personal purpose means not only for a leader to share his purpose with constituents but to allow others to be inspired to develop a personal purpose for themselves.

In one of Jim Collin's earlier books, *Built to Last: Successful Habits of Visionary Companies* (1994), the author compares the core purposes of IBM and Merck. He posits that if a company is going to withstand the test of time, a corporate purpose is needed that extends beyond economic or egotistical motives. IBM, known then for its computer business, had a purpose to make the best and sell the most mainframe computers in the world. The company realized its purpose. They were known in the 70s as 'Big Blue' and some considered IBM the cornerstone to the Dow Jones Industrial Average. At West Point, we had an IBM mainframe computer that filled up an entire classroom. I took a Fortran computer language class that required me to write computer programs using "data-cards." I could turn in my cards in the evening and get the results the next morning. Wow, so fast!

IBM continued to live for this purpose even after the mainframe computer was becoming obsolete. Eventually, IBM fell out of favor. From March 1st of 1973 to July 1st of 1975 their stock lost half its value. Their purpose was economically driven and short sighted. They assumed the mainframe computer would be the main force in technology indefinitely, but they were wrong. Their purpose failed to capture a future of change and innovation. Eventually, they changed their vision in order to survive, but the damage had already been done to investors, employees, and suppliers.

Merck, known for producing medicines and vaccines, has a purpose "to develop and provide innovative products and services that save and improve lives." They want to rid the world of disease. As long as the world has disease, they could continue their mission. Now, Merck has had their share of scandal and other challenges. They settled a seven billion dollar lawsuit over their drug Vioxx, a pain killer blamed for over 3,400 deaths due to the drug's cardiac side effects. Deceitful marketing, fake medical journals, and Medicaid fraud also cloud Merck's one hundred-year history in the United States. They drifted off course, losing sight of their purpose in favor of more short-sighted goals. Once they shifted back to realizing their purpose of ridding the world of disease, they were back on course and recovered. They remain a branded institution in their field.

Getting off course is a values dilemma; however, how can you have a course without a destination, or a purpose? I often ask myself, am I selling mainframe computers or trying to rid the world of disease? In other words, am I aligned with a short-sighted purpose driven by economics rather than a purpose that will extend itself beyond the fads and pressures of the present? Individuals, like companies, can drift off course but a core purpose will bring you back to your dedicated route.

Once you have established your core purpose, I would encourage you to change anything that does not contribute to its realization. Much has been written about transformation and change, but core to negotiating change is to define what does *not* change, and that is your core purpose. I would also encourage you to look at previous behaviors and decisions through the 'purpose' lens. Sometimes we do things that do not contribute to the realization of purpose, but you do not know until you have gained the experience. This relates to personal and group purpose. What a wonderful learning moment that can potentially contribute to future behaviors and decisions that will contribute to realizing your purpose.

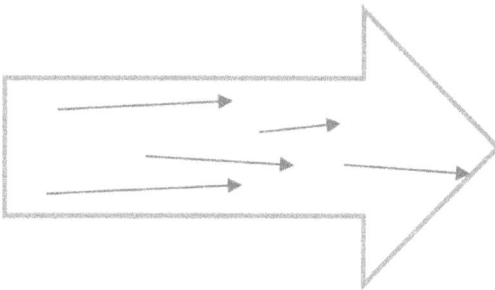

Note reference at the end of this section

8. Action Steps to Discovering and Aligning Purpose

Discovering your purpose is as basic to leadership as a destination is to a pilot's flight plan. This discovery is a process that demands an internal journey. Based on what you have read, let's take intentional steps towards your discovery.

1. What are the five most important things in your life?

2. As I mentioned in chapter 6, Bob Buford in his book *Halftime* suggests a personal inventory keying in on three categories. Buford shares what he views as the three categories of his life: family, religious beliefs, and career. What are your categories, and what are your dreams for each category? (Feel free to have less or more than three categories)

3. As I did with the streetsweeper, ask yourself no less than three times "Why is this important?" Each time you answer these questions, you will be further defining your purpose.

4. Step back, look at your answers, and write down your life's purpose.

5. Share your purpose with those you lead and take them

through the same inward journey articulated in steps 1-4.

6. Have everyone share their personal life's purpose.
7. What is the vision/purpose of the organization where you lead? All constituents should define how the group's purpose aligns with individual purposes (or not).
8. Write how your individual purpose is aligned with the group's purpose and express that to your teammates.

Now you have a better understanding of your starting point, where you and those you lead are today. You know what is important to each other, and you know each other's purpose. You also have a better understanding as to where you and the group are trying to get to. Let's now examine the instruments needed to keep you on course: values.

* *The idea of arrows representing individual purpose and aligned purpose originated in Peter Bregman's wonderful book Leading with Emotional Courage.*

Contributing Work
to Section 1

This work helped inspire some of the key concepts in this section

Bergman, P. (2018). *Leading With Emotional Courage*. Hoboken, New Jersey: Wiley & Sons, Inc.

Buford, Bob (Ed.) (1994, 2008). *Halftime: Changing Your Game Plan from Success to Significance* (ePub ed.). Grand Rapids, MI: Zondervan.

Collins, J., & Porras, J. (1994). *Built To Last: Successful Habits of Visionary Companies*. New York: Harper Collins.

Collins, J., & Porras, J. (1996). "Building Your Company's Vision," *Harvard Business Review*, September-October 1996, 12.

Duckworth, A. (2016). *Grit: The Power of Passion and Perseverance*. New York: Simon and Schuster.

Fiorina, C. (2006). *Tough Choices: A Memoir*. New York: Penguin Group, Inc.

Kouzes, J. M., & Posner, B. Z. (1995). *The Leadership Challenge: How to Get Extraordinary Things Done in Organizations*. San Francisco, CA: Jossey-Bass Publishers.

Turak, A. (2012). *The Trappist Way: Business Wisdom of the Trappist Monk*. Columbia University. Columbia, SC.

Section 2

Essential Instruments: Values

Group Culture: f(purpose, **values**)

The ideology, or culture, of any organization is a function of a unifying purpose and a **set of values that frame decisions and behaviors.**

Values not only fits into the culture of an organization; it is also a function of a leader's credibility. *Your credibility is a function of competence and being trusted.* Being trusted means that you have a set of values that you authentically express and model that are reasonably aligned with those you lead and the values that represent the group as a whole. Advertised values provide the consistency and predictability to a leader's behaviors and decisions that followers need. In other words, values provide stability.

This section will take you on a journey to discover or reaffirm your personal values, recognize the values of others, and the importance of personal values being aligned with the values of any group or organization you are affiliated with. While *purpose* defines your destination, *values* provide the instruments to guide you safely along the path towards that destination or purpose.

9. The Mellon Bank Story

As the new President of Mellon Bank Financial Advisors, I was excited about leading a group of professionals within one of the best-known financial institutions in the United States. I arrived on January 4, 2004, was processed in, and began meeting with my key employees. Specifically, I wanted to learn what I could do to help them become more successful. After many dinners and meetings, I discovered something troubling. It was evident that many advisors, now under my leadership, were not interested in helping the clients with important investment decisions, but rather were more focused on their own self interests. One financial advisor told me plainly, "We are an annuity company. All I will recommend is annuities and maybe an occasional mutual fund. Those are the products we get paid the most for. The sooner you learn that, the better it will be for all of us."

I also discovered that the division's marketing strategy included a brochure that listed numerous products and services we supposedly offered our clients. However, I was surprised, and disturbed, to discover that most of the products and services advertised on the brochure we could not offer. We were giving the client the impression we could do more than what we really could. It appeared to be a strategy to get people interested and then maneuver them to buy *what we could sell* rather than *what they really needed.*

I think the firm had intentions to eventually offer what they advertised. However, at the time, they gave our clients and me the impression the organization could do things they could not. My decision was simple; we either honor what the brochure represented or change the brochure.

I gave each manager responsibilities for developing products and services that were consistent with what we were representing to the public. The managers who reported to me did a good job, but those to whom I reported were not as supportive. My efforts were met with resistance. It became clear that the leadership above me was not in agreement. I became frustrated. It did not seem honest to portray something we could do knowing we could not. Despite my efforts to change this culture, the leadership above me would not support my position. I submitted my resignation.

Peter Drucker, in his famous article "Managing One's Self" writes, "To work in an organization whose value system is unacceptable or incompatible with one's own condemns a person both to frustration and nonperformance." Not only was I frustrated at the lack of support for my efforts to lead my group in a new direction, but I was also constrained from performing to the best of my abilities. I wasn't being allowed to lead from my values, I wasn't being the best leader I could be. The decision to leave this position was an easy one. I could not compromise my integrity by continuing to lead a group which said the best interest of the client comes first but didn't put that value into practice. My values were not aligned with the values of the organization.

After leaving the position, I received numerous calls of support and appreciation from other leaders in the financial industry that had some familiarity with the culture of this organization. These individuals recognized my efforts and saw how values drove my actions. Despite resigning and leaving the position, I still left an impact. This too serves as another testament to the power of leading with values. People notice and are impacted by your example.

To a leader of character, values are consciously considered in every decision and behavior. Ethical leaders of character behave and make decisions based on core values. Values are guiding lights that mark our ethical path and serve as an alarm clock when we stray. They provide us with the instruments needed to negotiate turbulence and remind us that *how* we do things is often as important as *what* we accomplish.

As an example, missed opportunities described in sponsoring 'Wine Over Water' in Chapter 4 may have been avoided if one of my values included 'Responsible Citizenship,' which it does today. The consequence of not discovering personal values lessens a leader's opportunity to realize one's full potential as a leader and may even lead to devastating results.

Group values are central to a group's identity. Groups could include organizations, workplaces, churches, and even families. Group values can be defined as the values associated with individual members that are similar and thus aligned. Coupled with a unifying purpose, group values form the culture of an organization. If group members have personal values that are reasonably aligned with the values that represent the group, then there can exist an expectation that these values will be considered in every decision, evaluation, hire, discussion, and so on. This consideration of values is what makes an organization an ethical agent.

So, how do we get there? We get there by leading our organizations with a strong unifying purpose and a set of shared values. We do so by first discovering personal values.

10. Consequences ... What Happened to Them?

Consequences of not discovering personal values may be devastating. Take the former governor of California, for example, who maintained two families, one for the public and one for his own private pleasure. Or consider the senator from South Carolina, who was a front runner for his party's nomination for President of the United States when details of a mistress were published, derailing his campaign. Both examples led to great family pain, including divorce. Then there was the governor and former attorney general of New York who touted taking down corruption and illegal activity but was personally involved with prostitutes.

And how can we forget the governor in Illinois who sold the appointment to a Senate seat previously occupied by the President of the United States? Sadly, he went to prison, just like four of the previous seven Illinois governors. By the way, for the politically astute, both major political parties have examples of leaders with a flawed value system.

The public sector is not alone with leaders void of selfless personal values. We have seen our corporate leaders negotiate self-serving agendas that allowed them to receive benefits and compensation beyond what they were entitled, and often commit fraud in the process. Bernie Madoff immediately comes to mind. Madoff was a former American market maker, investment advisor, and financier who died in 2021 while serving a federal prison sentence for offenses related to a massive Ponzi scheme. The scheme caused innocent people to lose millions of dollars. To some it was their entire life's savings.

Lately, a bevy of CEOs have been dismissed for demeaning behavior toward women; others face painful divorces due to their affairs becoming public. Behaviors like this can be found in all sectors and at all levels. These toxic behaviors are examples of a values crisis in our country.

People want to follow leaders who can help them accomplish things they want and need in life. They also want leaders who clearly believe in something wholesome and good. They long for leaders who have traveled within themselves to discover core beliefs that guide their behaviors and decisions. *I truly believe that people want leaders who are reflective, who have discovered their personal set of values, and who authentically articulate and model those values while respecting the values of others.*

II. Lead Yourself First

Earlier, I challenged you to differentiate the leader you respected, the selfless leader, versus the leader you did not respect, the self-serving leader. As far as self-serving leaders go, one person who comes to mind is Frank, an experienced leader at the same large international financial firm where I was a regional director. Frank was my boss. Frank tasked our team of directors with developing a business plan which would later be presented to Frank's boss and his staff. During the preparation, Frank and I respectfully disagreed on a particular matter. The matter had to do with recruiting, and it was something on which the team and I had researched and worked very hard.

Despite our efforts, Frank went with his idea. When he presented the plan to his boss and staff, with me and the rest of the team present, the matter over which Frank and I disagreed was debated. It became clear that the team's strategy was more favorably received than Frank's strategy. Frank responded by immediately adopting our idea and taking full personal credit for it. It became clear in that moment that Frank's agenda was self-enhancing, self-promoting, and self-serving.

Have you ever had someone take credit for your work and accomplishment at your expense? Have you ever had to report to a leader whose primary value was to serve himself? That was Frank. I had no idea what Frank's personal values were, nor did Frank have any interest in mine. I think it was just assumed that our values were what the firm told us they were according to the corporate short-term objectives. Frank was allowing himself to be led by values that were not his, and thus were not authentic. He rationalized decisions and behaviors based on what was best for him.

Frank was eventually replaced by Rob, and during that leadership transition, my wife died. My two daughters, sixteen and nineteen years old respectively, and I were going through a painful transition. Professionally, I was still leading the same large region in the central part of the country, and things were not going very well. The division's annuity business was struggling. I felt my team needed some concrete ideas that I was not providing.

My new boss, Rob, came to me with an idea. Rob developed a system that inspired financial advisors to communicate with their clients monthly. His idea was so simple, yet brilliant: simply ask the financial advisors on their monthly client calls to ask their customers if they owned an annuity. The theory was that the financial advisors were unaware of the annuities owned by many of their clients, and many of those annuities were outdated. A simple comparison of other options like moving the money to a better annuity could improve the client's financial position while generating significant revenue for the firm.

Rob coached me through introducing and testing the idea. I began to receive calls from financial advisors thanking me for the suggestion. It was extremely simple and extremely successful. Some months later, Rob was giving a speech to the entire management team explaining why we were so successful with our annuity business. He concluded his speech by saying, "And John came up with this great idea and executed it flawlessly. Let's give John applause for such great work." He gave full credit to me and took none for himself.

Rob was courageous, confident, competent, smart, but, most importantly, selfless. I knew Rob's purpose, "To release the human potential choosing growth over fear." I also know one of Rob's values was "helping others". That value resonated with me, and he and I connected. Our values and purpose were aligned.

12. Reflection on Your Past

A Young Captain's Story

I knew a young captain in the Army who had four lieutenants that reported to him. This captain would call a weekly meeting of his lieutenants and consistently be ten or fifteen minutes late. The captain's attitude was that he could be late for his own meeting because, after all, it could not start until he got there. When the captain entered the office late, the lieutenants would look at their watch and then glanced at each other as if to say, "Here we go again." The lieutenants interpreted their captain's constant tardiness as a lack of respect for their time and position. That captain was me.

To be critical of Frank (or yourself) is fair as long as the intent is not to be necessarily critical but rather to learn and reflect on where one could be better. This journey inward can be painful, but these reflections can be invaluable in discovering the values that you want to guide your behaviors and decisions.

As I mentioned earlier, I sometimes wonder what would be said about me by those I have led. Would they put me in the category of the leader most respected, or the one they least respected? I wonder how those young lieutenants would judge me. Probably they would put me on the list reserved for the least respected leader. While those mistakes are in the past and cannot be changed, when reflected on today, they become wonderful learning opportunities. I know now that those mistakes may have been avoided if I was intentional about framing a set of personal values that tested decisions and behaviors as being right or wrong, like a filter. It may have prevented doing something that was wrong by rationalizing it to be right. The future is up to us to shape the kind of leaders we want to be. What will frame your decisions and behaviors of the future?

Buford would want us to reflect on the first half of life similar to the inward journey I am asking you to take. In my first half, I remember my dreams of being an NBA basketball player, an accomplished military officer, and a wealthy financial businessman. My values reflected what I thought was important, and like Frank, they centered on me. Then I got married and became a father. My values were impacted by what were the most important things, but my list of what was most important changed over time. It was becoming less about me and more about others. Today one of my values is "Respect for the Individual." I think if I had a weekly meeting with those lieutenants today, I would respect their time by being on time myself.

13. What Do You Believe In?

Leaders often answer questions or make decisions that pertain to beliefs. Do you allow a constituent to attend his son's championship baseball game, thus excusing him from an important meeting? Should you apologize for being late to your own meeting? What do you say to a new leader who reports to you on his first day? What do you say when confronted with off-color jokes or comments? How do you explain denying a request that contradicts what you believe in? It is the aim of this book to help you answer questions like these. By now, you should already understand your purpose. Yet, discovering your values is equally important.

After reflecting on my own personal experiences and studies, I concluded that first, bad behavior and decisions often arise from a life purpose that is primarily focused on serving self rather than serving others. As discussed in Section One, a life's purpose keeps us pointed in a 'good' direction. A leader without a wholesome purpose will have a greater opportunity to rationalize bad behavior and poor decisions as opposed to a leader who has a purpose that extends beyond self-serving motives.

Secondly, selfish or unwholesome decisions and behaviors emerge where a strong value system is absent. A strong set of personal and corporate values can deter evil behavior. Values serve as reminders that can keep us on course or get us back on course to realizing our purpose. Core values will not be intimidated by shortsighted economic or egotistical objectives. They serve as a checklist, similar to a pilot's check list, which is used to bring clarity of action during difficult or challenging times.

Third, a strong set of values that are authentically expressed and modeled will lessen the effects of dysfunctions that make the leader less effective. A strong value system gives the leader the confidence to make right decisions, even when it may be difficult.

It took some maturity, and yes, some failures for me to appreciate that our followers want leaders that believe in something that is wholesome and good. What would you say if someone were to ask, *What do you believe in*? In this world of constant change, what is the common thread that frames your decisions and behaviors? Can your followers count on you to give some degree of stability and trust in what you are?

What I respected in Rob was something that was missing in Frank: a clear set of values that included helping others. This inspired me to think about the values that guide my decisions and my behavior. What is my character? How can I expect to lead others without being able to lead myself?

Personal values are at the center of leading yourself, as well as leading others, and are essential equipment for effective leadership. Personal values are core to everything. Discovering and using personal values is no different than learning to use the instruments necessary to keeping a pilot on course. Again, when turbulence is encountered, a pilot relies on instruments to stay on course. A selfless and effective leader with wholesome personal values that once discovered, authentically expressed, and modeled are essential for successfully negotiating the turbulence of difficult times. Values define a leader's character.

Consider the metaphor of a pilot's flight plan. People who consistently make poor decisions or behave inappropriately do not have the instruments (values) or do not know how to use the instruments that would keep them on course. Could it be they have not discovered their personal core values (instruments)? If not, what platform does a leader use to dictate behaviors and decisions that guide their course except for their own desires and needs, independent of the desires and needs of those they lead?

Or, what thought has been committed to purpose (where the instruments are taking them)? I suspect that the difference between the leaders we respect versus leaders we do not respect is often whether the leader has discovered a wholesome set of values that serve as a baseline for behaviors and decisions. Without this discovery, there is no baseline that frames the consistency needed by followers from their leaders.

What do I admire in my leaders and what do I despise? Ask yourself: *What is important to me? What guides my decisions and behaviors? Have I been serious about discovering and defining my personal values? What are my values? Have I conducted an inward journey to discover my values?* This personal discovery is essential to your character as a leader. Effective leadership demands that leaders answer the simple question "What do you believe in?"

Let's find your answer; your followers deserve to know, whether they be employees, church members, or your own children.

14. An Inward Journey

Why We Do Things

The financial firm where I served as a regional director made a strategic decision to become a wealth management institution. This was a sound idea that is still in effect today. Embedded in this strategy was the authoring of a financial plan for each client that would orchestrate all their finances. The plan included risk assessment, asset allocation, estate planning, some tax planning, retirement planning, college planning, and so on. The revenue potential for the firm was enormous. It benefited the clients in that all their finances would be orchestrated by one institution, simplifying the client's financial life. So far, so good.

The strategy was easy to support. Financial advisors and managers like me were rewarded for the number of financial plans they processed. Within the first year of launching the strategy, I won a trip to England because my operation did more financial plans than any other. Financial advisors would win trips and prizes for completing a certain number of plans. Since a manager's success was partially measured by the number of plans their operations did, some managers chose to threaten financial advisors with their jobs for not doing enough plans. One advisor, who was desperate after being threatened, called a client who was a good friend and told him of his situation. The friend said he would complete a financial plan to help his friend. When the advisor asked for pertinent financial information to ensure the plan's accuracy the friend/client said, "Just put down anything you want. *Make it up!* Save your job."

On reflection, I ask myself, *Why did I support this strategy, the shift to wealth management and financial planning? Was it recognition, increased pay, or to save my job?* Though these can be effective motivators, I would hope that the underlining motivator would be a more selfless motive of doing what is best for the client. I would hope that the motives for financial planning was to create real change that was client centered. I am sure for many it was, but for some, the more self-serving motives were the primary reason for the focus.

Many financial advisors were not competent to interpret the information the plans provided. They were well trained to handle the investments, but for many advisors, the other dynamics included in the plan were outside their level of expertise.

As the new initiative rolled out, some attempts were made to educate the advisors on financial planning, along with hiring consultants. Unfortunately for many that effort was secondary to getting the financial plan document itself published. Financial plans kept pouring in, and financial advisors and their managers kept winning trips and recognition. New bookcases were purchased to store the plans. Too many times these plans were never really used to help the client and did nothing more than collect dust.

Despite the self-serving motives, some managers and advisors realized on their own that being client-focused meant being intellectually competent and thus were motivated to use the plans to help their clients. They became Certified Financial Planners or formed a team with tax advisors and estate attorneys. For some, the 'why' to financial planning was to serve the client to help them accomplish life goals. For others, the 'why' to financial planning was recognition and personal compensation. For some, the motive to do financial plans was transformational and focused on the best interest of the client, but for others the motive was more transactional and focused on more self-serving motives. One of the values of the firm was "Client Focused." The problem was that this value (along with the other values of Respect for the Individual, Integrity, Teamwork, and Responsible Citizenship) were not imbedded in the organization's culture to the degree they impacted leadership's behaviors and decisions.

Years later, during the financial crisis, this firm ceased to exist on their own and had to be taken over. I and many others believe the reason for the firm's demise as a stand-alone corporation was its leadership's failure, starting with the firm's CEO, to make decisions and behave according to these values.

Some years later, as a Senior Vice-President for another major international financial firm, I was responsible for leading financial advisors in Florida. The emphasis on financial planning was like my previous experience with one exception: I was operating from a firm set of personal values that included "the best interest of the client comes first." Rather than having contests or being coercive to inspire more financial plans, we inspired financial planning through education. I hired an accredited professor to teach courses that would prepare managers and financial advisors to pass the required tests to be awarded the Certified Financial Planner designation.

The education was strictly voluntary, but I was pleased to see that it was very popular, with participation from not only my region but neighboring offices not under my responsibility. This effort inspired participants to support financial planning efforts because they understood the value the effort could bring to their clients. Financial plans were completed, not because of internal recognition, increased pay, or coercive threats. They were done because the financial advisors had increased knowledge and were motivated to use their expertise to truly help their clients and not just themselves.

An inward journey requires an honest reflection as to the 'why' we do something rather than the 'what' we do. Does a politician seek votes out of service or to get reelected? Does a pastor give a sermon to spread God's word or to 'fill the seats? Does a business person measure success by financial gain and recognition or by a selfless motive to benefit something more than just self? Does a financial advisor recommend a financial plan to a client because of their own self-serving agenda, or do they recommend a financial plan because it is a valuable tool to help their client?

An inward journey can reveal a personal set of values that can be the core to wholesome decisions and behaviors. Discovering your values starts with discovering, through reflection, what is important to you. We did this in Chapter 1. After reviewing that list, we can begin our inward journey to discover how we frame decisions and behaviors—discovering our core personal values.

15. Discovering Your Values

Self-awareness is central to discovering values and requires an intentional effort of personal self-reflection. This effort journeys through previous experiences, both good and bad. This is an important part of Buford's 'halftime' of life. It challenges us to identify what our most meaningful, energizing, enriching, and enjoyable experiences are. Imagine what you want your legacy to be. Now, imagine disappearing today. How would you be remembered, or how would you hope to be remembered?

Effective leadership encourages us not to be afraid of confronting mistakes or behaviors we may not be proud of, while appreciating decisions and behaviors that make us proud. It is part of the inner work that will move us to discovering the core values that frame our behaviors. This book seeks to challenge us to courageously and honestly travel inward to discover what we truly value. This inward reflection is critically important to effective leadership. These discovered core values will frame our future decisions and behaviors and thus are critically important to effective leadership.

Take time to deeply reflect as you answer these questions:

1. If you owned a business and were leaving for six months and could not communicate with your direct reports during that time, what would you say to them in ad-

vance? Picture them in front of you now. You need to give them guidance as to what you expect in your absence. How do you want them to make decisions and guide the company in your absence?

2. If you were to start a new organization in a different line of work, what core values would you build into the new organization, regardless of the industry?

3. If you had one hour to live and you had the most important people in your life in front of you, what would you say? What you say they will never forget. It is what will guide them during their tough times. It will be your legacy and be repeated to people they deeply love.

* * *

Reflect on your answers. Now, write down your core values. Limit the list from three to six core values. More can be confusing, while fewer may not provide enough framing or discipline to guide good decisions and behaviors. It can be beneficial in this process of discovering personal beliefs and values to enlist others for help and receive feedback from trusted associates.

Discussions with those close to you may play a pivotal role in discovering these values.

Questions from someone you trust can bring further clarity in how to apply these values. These are your personal guides for every decision and behavior. They will seldom, if ever, change. Here are a few of the most popular values I have discovered when conducting Values Based Leadership workshops:

Integrity	Patriotism
Spiritual centeredness	Being customer focused
Stewardship	Excellence
Responsible citizenship	Putting people first
Connectedness	Trustworthiness
Teamwork	Hard work
Respect for others	Quality work
Stick-to-itiveness	Positivity
Innovation	Having fun
Charity first	Being family focused
Continued Creativity	Doing one's best
Loyalty	Christ centered
Respect for the individual	Be kind

Once you have discovered your core values as a leader, you need to express them in your own words. This is an authentic expression of your beliefs and what you stand for. You will try to model them in everything you do. These values will define you, show what you care about, and truly express *who* you are.

Once a leader has explored his/her inner self and can define what he/she cares about, what defines her, and what makes him who he is, then personal core values will have been discovered. Effective leaders then give opportunities for followers and constituents to conduct a similar inward journey, to discover and express their personal values. Only when everyone has journeyed inward to discover core values and expressed them honestly can we begin to discover group or organizational values.

16. Defining Each Value

The United States Military Academy at West Point has an honor code that states, "a cadet will not lie, cheat, or steal, or tolerate anyone who does." It is not uncommon for other institutions to have an honor code without the toleration clause. For example, at the United States Naval Academy, their honor code, known as the Honor Concept, prohibits midshipmen from lying, cheating, and stealing. These academies are two of the most honorable institutions I know. I have a son who graduated from the Naval Academy, and as I mentioned earlier, I graduated from West Point.

The Naval Academy does not have a specific toleration clause like West Point, though I may argue it is implied. I definitely do not imply that the Naval Academy's honor code is inferior to West Point's honor code. It is not; however, as a cadet at West Point, if I observe another cadet cheating, I am required to turn that person in, and if I do not, I am as guilty as the cheater. It is how honor and integrity are defined.

It is nice to know how integrity or honor is defined before one attends these academies or any organization where 'integrity' is a value. Without a clear definition, people will spin their own definition, hence it is defined according to the individual rather than the organization. A candidate for admittance to either institution should determine if they are aligned with the core values and their definitions before accepting an invitation to attend. So, it should be with any candidate for any organization.

Most people and organizations include 'honesty' or 'integrity' as one of their core values. I know I do. However, like the Naval Academy and the US Military Academy, definitions can vary. Like our other discussions on purpose and values, it starts with me, or you, the leader. How do you define integrity? How do the organizations you lead define integrity? And finally, how do your constituents define integrity?

This discovery process must be applied to each core value. It is not enough to discover core values with a phrase or word. The core value must be wrapped with meaning and clarity. At the service academies it is clear: do not lie, cheat, or steal. In addition, at West Point, you are not to tolerate anyone whom you know has violated the honor code. Anyone who attends these institutions knows the code; there is no debate. I would argue that all leaders owe this kind of clarity in defining each core value to their followers.

Another core value we often discover is "Respect for the Individual." So, what does this mean? That we respect different views? That we respect different backgrounds? That we respect individuals even when conflict occurs? That we should respect someone who does not respect us or our values? All these questions deserve some clarity.

A definition could be "At XYZ corporation, respect for the individual means that we respect our differences and look at our differences as opportunities to discover the best solutions for complex problems. We celebrate what makes each member of our team special and we welcome opportunities to learn and grow as people and professionals."

This definition helps clarify how XYZ Corporation approaches conflict and how teammates look at each other. The employees of XYZ Corporation have clarity. They know that conflict is an opportunity for a better solution and that every member of the team should be looking for opportunities to celebrate the greatness of teammates. They also know that learning and growing opens the door for conversations that sometimes may be difficult, but are in the context of helping someone or something be better. These definitions provide clarity as to how employees are expected to behave and make decisions.

Defining group core values can be an opportunity to inspire collaboration and to help team members gain a greater appreciation for how they can impact the culture of the team. As an exercise, have each of your team members reflect on each core value and write how they would define it. Then, have each member read their definitions to the group. After a discussion, try to agree on a definition that can represent each value. Each definition will be a reminder on keeping the organization on a course (the instruments) to arrive at its destination (realizing its purpose).

This collaboration does not mean that full agreement will be realized. On the contrary, some may only have partial alignment with the group's agreed upon values and definitions. In rare cases, some individuals may have little alignment of values, like Stan O'Neal, the CEO at Merrill Lynch (upcoming story in Chapter 17), or me at Mellon Bank. Constituents with significantly different core values or different definitions are probably frustrated and will eventually leave. These departures provide an opportunity to hire someone with not only the necessary talent and skill to do the job, but also with personal values aligned with team values. I would additionally hope that anyone leaving a position would find an environment more aligned with their individual values. I know I did.

17. Affirming and Aligning Values Brings Support and Unity

Affirming means to provide emotional support and encouragement. Once personal values are discovered by all, leaders then must affirm those values. By doing so, leaders give support and appreciation for what each person represents in such a way that encourages and embeds a sense of confidence within followers. This goes beyond recognizing people's accomplishments. It is an acceptance of a person's core beliefs. Because of this affirmation of people's values, followers not only believe in their leaders, but, more importantly, they believe in themselves. When values are reasonably aligned, appreciation for each other's values forms an alliance between leader and follower that allows that partnership to accomplish things far beyond what would take place in the absence of such an alliance.

Affirming the Values of Others

Recall someone who really cared about you. I am not talking about relatives like your mother, father, brother, or sister. I am talking about someone you worked with or reported to that you knew *really* cared about you. Maybe you recall a boss, teacher, coach, pastor, or peer. Now, how did you know that person cared? Was it through words of encouragement? Was it through recognition? Was it a sincere interest in your future? Maybe this person showed great support when you really needed it?

I remember Arv Watt, my old high school basketball coach. I remember crying after losing a big game. Coach Watt wrapped his arms around me and told me he loved me and that he was proud of me. I knew he cared. I remember Colonel Hannas, my German professor at West Point. I struggled in this class. Colonel Hannas never missed an opportunity to encourage me and compliment me in the class — even when I fumbled through my words. Upon graduating, he sent me a note of congratulations. He did not have to do that. He cared.

I remember Rob, my boss when I was a director for Merrill Lynch. Things were not going well after my wife died, and he gave me that brilliant idea that proved to be very successful. Remember, in front of peers and superiors, he gave me full credit for his idea and its execution. He did not have to do that, but he did. He cared.

All these leaders had the following in common: they understood what I cared about and what was important to me, and they all cared about me and showed that caring by providing emotional support and encouragement for my behaviors and decisions. It was my values that guided those decisions and behaviors. Their support and encouragement affirmed my values.

One of the most important traits of effective leadership is understanding the values of other people. We understand how important it is for leaders to have a set of personal values that are authentically expressed and modeled. It is equally important to allow followers the space to express what is important to them and what values guide their behaviors and decisions. The values of an organization are not necessarily the leader's values, or the values stated on a brochure. Maybe these are the values we would like to see in our organization, but they are not always embedded in the culture.

Discovering the values of an organization must include a process of discovering personal values of every individual and then determining the values common to most of the participants. The process of personal values discovery, expressing those values, and then listing, and affirming the values most commonly expressed is significant evidence to the core values of the group. The process of discovering what is valued by our constituents could be the critical component to inspiring and showing the caring that everyone needs. It also could reveal values that are important to continue and values that need revision or changing.

In the movie *The Blind Side* (based on a real-life story), Sandra Bullock plays the part of Leigh Anne Tuohy, mother to an adopted son Michael Oher. Both Mrs. Tuohy and her husband were formidable athletes in their day. Given Michael's unusually large size, they had hopes he would develop into a good football player as an offensive lineman and even play at their alma mater, Ole' Miss. There is a problem however. Despite Michael's size, he initially is not at all aggressive in protecting the quarterback or running backs, which is his job as an offensive lineman.

In the movie, Michael's high school football coach, Coach Cotton, played by Ray McKinnon, chastises Michael for his lack of aggressiveness. Leigh Anne, upon observing this forceful exchange, interrupts practice by walking on to the field to have a conversation with her son. She reminds Michael how he protected her when they were in a bad side of town and how he stopped the airbag from hurting his brother during a traffic accident. She explains to Michael that the football team is like a family, and it needed to be protected as well.

Michael's football demeanor instantly changes — for the better. Later, Burt (Coach Cotton) asks Leigh Anne what she had said. She informs him that due to his difficult past Michael had protective instincts and did not trust men who yell at him. Then she says, "You should get to know your players, Burt."

As leaders, we should get to know our players. Specifically, we should work to know what is important to them, and we should work to know the personal core values that form the basis for their decisions and behaviors.

I would encourage you to spend time posing those questions to your constituents that I posed earlier. I would also advise you to authentically express your answers to those questions. You will be amazed at what you will learn independent of how long you have worked with someone. Again, here are the questions, with some additions:

1. What core values (values that you would hold regardless of whether they were rewarded) do you personally bring to your work?
2. What core values would you tell your children that you hold at work and that you hope they will hold as working adults?
3. If you were to start a new organization in a different line of work, what core values would you build into the new organization regardless of the industry?
4. If you had one hour to live and you had the most important people in your life in front of you, what would

you say? What you say they will never forget. It is what will guide them during their tough times. It will be your legacy and be repeated to people they deeply love.

Aligning Values

Merrill Lynch was founded in 1914 by Charles Merrill and Edmund Lynch. The company grew into a massive retail brokerage institution that aimed to introduce everyday investors to the stock market, and its brokers became known as the "thundering herd." Over the years, the firm's leaders took pride in living by a set of five values: Client-Centered, Respect for the Individual, Integrity, Teamwork, and Responsible Citizenship.

As a leader in the firm, these values significantly influenced the forming of my personal values. However, during the financial crisis of 2008, it was clear Merrill Lynch could not survive on its own. Bank of America, under pressure from the US Department of Treasury, bought Merrill Lynch. Hence Merrill Lynch was no longer a standalone company. Some feel that this occurred because Merrill Lynch leadership abandoned the values that steered their decisions and behaviors.

In addressing the board of directors of Merrill Lynch on December 6, 2008, Wynn Smith, former vice-chairman, and son of one of the firm's founders, reflected on the recent demise of Merrill Lynch as a standalone company. Smith stated that in the fall of 2001 he was asked by the new CEO, Stan O'Neal, to stay on as Vice-Chairman; however, after a private meeting with the CEO, Smith resigned his position and ended a thirty-five-year career.

Smith stated, "In a private meeting it was obvious that this

CEO had no respect for our history, for our culture, and for the five principles [values] that had served us so well." Smith concluded that the corporate values that guided the firm for many years were not aligned with O'Neal's values. In fact, it was unclear what values even defined O'Neal.

Several years later, O'Neal's maneuvering of resources for personal gain became well known. To use Smith's words to the Board of Directors, "Shame on you for allowing a CEO to surround himself with many people who did not share the same values that made us great and appreciate a winning culture." Smith, in his self-published history about Merrill Lynch wrote that O'Neal and his management team "allowed short-term profitability to blind their views of the highly leveraged and risky business Merrill would become, and they allowed a small group of greedy individuals to destroy an icon." O'Neal replaced many long-standing employees, cut costs severely, over-leveraged the firm, and cluttered the balance sheet with waste that gave the appearance of profit. He openly professed that the corporate values were not his values. Some believe that O'Neal's primary purpose was consumed with increasing his personal wealth, which is represented in the $161 million retirement package he was granted. The evidence suggests that the firm's demise was not only bad timing due to the economy, but an absence of alignment between the established values of the firm and the personal values of the leadership, thus causing the firm to drift off course.

The values of an organization rest in the values that are generally aligned between leaders, followers, peers, and any constituent associated with the organization. Group values are the aligned values of every manager, floor sweeper, secretary, or president. Leaders cannot order constituents to adopt a certain set of values any more than leaders can adopt core values around certain positions or places. Personal core values do not change because of a new job or affiliation, but they can evolve.

Constituents may appreciate the group's values only if they have discovered their own values and can appreciate some, or all, of those values being realized within the group they work or serve in. If leaders want to create a culture around a certain set of values, they must encourage their constituents to conduct the inward journey previously described. Only upon that discovery and authentic expression of the values by everyone, leader, and follower, can alignment, or misalignment, be discovered.

18. Affirmed and Aligned Values Bring Unity and Support

Leaders do not just speak for themselves; they speak for everyone under their watch. Hence, leaders must reach out to discover, and hopefully appreciate, the values of others. If leaders desire to bring unity to groups or organizations, they must recognize the personal values of those that follow, and they must celebrate the alignment of personal values with group values. This unity cannot be ordered or forced, rather, leaders must give constituents reasons to care. The caring that produces unity is a product of affirmed shared values. A values-driven culture provides an understanding between leader and follower that is the glue in unification and trust. Failure to do this can bring devastating consequences.

The Ruthless Hire and a Transformed Culture

Part of my responsibility in leading a region for a large financial company was to improve the revenue. That meant improving revenue for an office located in the central part of Tennessee that had been performing poorly for some time. To help remedy the situation, I hired a financial advisor who, despite having a ruthless reputation, also had a history of being very productive. My thought was that this injection of revenue would improve the office's overall profits while inspiring others to perform better. The opposite happened. The higher producing advisor only sold products with the highest commissions, even though one of our core values was, "The best interests of the client come first."

In hiring this person, I unknowingly sent a signal that short-term results were more important than honoring values. Fortunately, within a year, that person left. I eventually hired a manager for the office that understood that the best interests of the client must come first. This time, I was careful to hire someone with aligned values. Performance finally started to improve.

When values are intentionally discovered and aligned, unity will evolve, and wonderful things can happen. Several years ago, I was asked to speak and conduct leadership workshops in my local area's 911 communication center. The first workshop included three shift leaders with their respective team leaders and the training division, to include the Director of Training, the Director of Human Resources, the Chief Operations Officer, and the Executive Director. The group totaled about twenty-five, and they were the principal leaders of the organization.

It did not take long to discover that a significant lack of trust, an unhealthy questioning of leadership, and a culture of "doing your own thing" rather than working toward a unifying effort focused on a wholesome purpose was contaminating the culture. In one of the small group discussions, one of the team members refused to participate and was openly insubordinate to her boss.

In another small group discussion, it was apparent that the shift leader was disregarding the guidance from the Executive Director and was persistent in doing it "his way and his way only." Leadership displayed a lack of respect for their peers and followers alike.

The group was asked to answer the questions I posed earlier. In answering those questions and through the discussions that followed, private agendas revealed themselves, personal conflicts were exposed, and it was clear there was a serious morale problem that was negatively affecting the culture of the entire organization. It was also clear that, for some, the newly discovered personal values were not aligned with what the group agreed to as the group's values.

After the initial workshops, the Executive Director settled on five values that would represent the organization in the future:

Integrity: Do the right thing at the right time for the right reasons

Respect for the Individual: Treat each other with dignity and understanding while respecting our differences

Teamwork: Bring the skills of individuals together as a coordinated team to accomplish the mission

Dependability: Do what you say you are going to do

Callers and First Responders Centered: Our duty is to rally resources and efforts in support of callers and first responders

We worked with the entire leadership team to come up with the definition for each value. We then developed an intentional process to promote, hire, coach, and sometimes terminate leaders whose values were not appropriately aligned with the organization's values. People left and were replaced with people who shared these values. After several years, the leaders of the organization became unified, looking to each other for support and guidance. Morale has improved and the culture is now transformed. We are now developing intentional efforts to further embed these values throughout the entire organization.

There were several keys to the success of this effort. First, the Executive Director, along with the principal management team, understood that a purpose-based and values-driven organization was a key component to evolving the culture toward a favorable workplace. Second, collaboration with the *entire* management team in deciding on the values inspired a spirit of teamwork. Third, embedding the desired values among leaders were prioritized before impressing those values upon the entire organization. Finally, a structured process was included in future hiring, coaching, and promoting.

Specifically, in the next promotion board where twenty-three people were assessed to occupy six vacant leadership positions, values alignment was a major portion of the assessment. Also, the structured interviews conducted for new hires were adjusted to assess personal values of the candidate and their alignment with the organization's values.

Creating a culture based on a set of core values takes time and patience. It takes coaching (as we will see in Section 4), recognition, hiring, promoting, and sometimes losing those whose individual values are not aligned. Failing to create a culture driven by core group values can devastate an organization. It causes frustration, hurts morale, and loses good employees.

Creating a values-driven culture requires replacing employees whose personal values are not aligned with people with like values to the group or organization. It took almost two years to transform the 911 Communications Center to a culture that is positive and encouraging. However, the success was realized only after the organization's values were determined and the leadership articulated and modeled those values through their own behaviors and decisions. A natural process of hiring, promoting, and recognizing employees who follow these values ensued and the culture shifted in a wonderful way.

19. Values-Based Hiring, Promoting, and Recognition

My hiring of the ruthless financial advisor in central Tennessee, my accepting a position with Mellon Bank, and my experience with the 911 communication center should resonate on three levels. First, organizations need to be intentional about hiring people whose personal values are somewhat aligned with the organization's values. Often the selection criterion for new hires focuses primarily on skill sets. Evaluating skills based on education, previous experience, and even the questioning of references is sensible. However, that evaluation should not come at the expense of efforts to intentionally discover their values and assess their alignment with the organization's values. Case in point, if I would have assessed the values of the financial advisor hired in Middle Tennessee, I probably would not have hired him.

Second, hiring is a two-way street. Candidates should assess whether the organization's values are consistent with values that they can represent. Certainly, analysis of position, pay, and supervisor are important, but *equally important* is the responsibility of candidates to assess the alignment between their personal values and the values that represent the organization's leadership. I had evidence prior to being hired at Mellon Bank (Chapter 12) that my supervisor at the bank had a different definition of integrity than did I. Despite that evidence, I took the position. Upon reflection, I should have politely declined.

Third, once values have been discovered and leadership has decided what values will represent the organization, an intentional effort can be made to assess personal values when not only hiring, but also promoting and recognizing significant contributions to the organization. Today the 911 center has a cohesive group of leaders that were promoted into those positions primarily because of their aligned values. The morale of the organization has significantly improved because of these promotions. Contributions supporting established values will be met with recognition and reward. Contributions not supporting established values should be met with coaching and/or some form of discipline.

Values Are More Than a Marketing Tool

One mistake that organizations sometimes make is they assume that marketing their values in a brochure or displaying their values on signs will, by themselves, produce a values-driven culture. This is akin to placing learning objectives on a blackboard and assuming students will learn through osmosis. It doesn't work like that. Nor can values be forced from the top down. Values cannot be used as rules. They aren't ideas to "comply" with. Instead, they need to be authentically embraced and shared by stakeholders. Though efforts to display values, or to guide personnel to embody values may be well intentioned, they are not enough by themselves.

Openly advertising desired values can have the desired impact *if* that advertisement is a compliment to other intentional efforts (some previously mentioned) supporting organizational values. Coaching, rewarding, hiring, and releasing constituents are powerful messages to everyone, employees, and customers alike, that the organization is values-driven. With these efforts the brochures and signs are helpful. Without these efforts the brochures and signs are but a marketing tool with little cultural impact. The real marketing occurs when members of your team live the values that their organizations represent. People notice and want to be a part of such organizations.

20. Action Steps for Discovering, Aligning, and Defining Values

The character of an organization is the degree in which values are used as principal guides to behaviors and decisions. The ideology of an organization is the alignment of efforts towards purpose while adhering to a set of values that frame decisions and behaviors. An organization's character is embedded in the character of its leaders.

Action steps begin at the starting point: you. First you must intentionally discover your core values. This is followed by asking constituents to participate by discovering and advertising their values. It is the responsibility of the leader to find the common values within the group, revise those values where the leader deems appropriate and then, with group collaboration, define each value.

Discovering Your Personal Values

Ask yourself the following questions and write your answers.
1. List the five most important priorities in your life.

2. What core values (values that you would hold regardless of whether they were rewarded) do you personally bring to your work?
3. What core values would you tell your children that you hold at work and that you hope they will hold as working adults?
4. If you were to start a new organization in a different line of work, what core values would you build into the new organization regardless of the industry.
5. If you had one hour to live and you had the most important people in your life in front of you, what would you say? What you say they will never forget. It is what will guide them during their tough times. It will be your legacy and be repeated to people they deeply love.

Look carefully at your answers and write down your personal values.

Discovering Constituents Values

Ask the same questions to constituents and have them write their answers and read their answers to you and their team. Read your answers to them.

Have them reflect on their answers and then write down and share their values.

Look for common themes that may provide evidence of core group values.

Adapt or revise values from the common themes.

Building Group Core Values

If you were to start a new organization in a different line of work, what core values would you build into your new organization regardless of industry?

What are the current values of the group? These would be the common themes in the previous step.

What core values does the group need to adapt to ensure a bright future?

What are the group's core values? (At this point the leader may step up and proclaim the values of the organization that will lead them into the future).

Defining Each Value

1. In twenty-five words or less, have each participant personally define each value. Take them one at a time.
2. Each participant is to read their value and as a group discuss and attempt to reach consensus on each values definition.
3. With this input, the leader is to step up and provide to the group the organization's values with definition.

Embed Values into the Organization

1. Institute intentional process in transforming the organization according to these values
2. Inspire transformational leadership while being informed by these values (see Section 3)
3. Coach using these values as a centerpiece (see Section 4).

4. Motivate constituents using purpose and values as a basis for these efforts (see Section 5).

Contributing Work
to Section 2

The following works helped inspire some of the key concepts

Cosgrove, J. F. (2016). *The Impact of Values Clarification and Expression of Beliefs on Dysfunctional Leadership Among Church Lay Leaders*. (Doctor of Philosophy), Andrews University, Berrien Springs, MI.

Kouzes, J. M., & Posner, B. Z. (2012). *The Leadership Challenge: How to Make Extraordinary Things Happen in Organizations* (5 ed.). San Francisco, CA: Jossey-Bass.

George, B. and P. Sims (2007). *True North: Discover Your Authentic Leadership*. San Francisco, CA, Jossey-Bass.

Palmer, P. (2000). *Let Your Life Speak: Listening for the Voice of Vocation*. San Francisco, Josey-Bass, Inc.

Buford, B., Ed. (1994, 2008). *Halftime: Changing Your Game Plan from Success to Significance*. Grand Rapids, MI, Zondervan.

Drucker, P. (1999). "Managing Oneself." *Harvard Business Review*: 13.

Smith, W. (December 6, 2008). Speech by Win Smith (as in Merrill Lynch Pierce Fenner and Smith). Merrill Lynch Annual Meeting to Stockholders, Princeton, NJ, Guest Author.

Drucker, P. (1999). "Managing Oneself." *Harvard Business Review*: 13.

Cooper, T. D. (2006). *Making Judgements without Being Judgmental*. Madison, WI: InterVarsity Press.

Covey, S. R. (1997). *The 7 Habits of Highly Effective Families*. New York: Franklin Covey Company.

Johnson, C. (2012). *Meeting the Ethical Challenge of Leadership: Casting Light or Shadow* (4 ed.). Thousand Oaks, CA: Sage Publications, Inc.

Martin, & Roger. (2009). "The Opposable Mind Winning through Integrative Thinking." Boston: *Harvard Business Review*.

Collins, J. (2005). *Good to Great in the Social Sectors*. Chicago: Collins Publisher.

Ibid.

Devalia, A. (2008). *Personal Social Responsibility* (First ed.). St. John's Wood, London: Nirvana Publishing.

Greenleaf. (2002). *Servant Leadership: A Journey into the Nature of Legitimate Power and Greatness* (25th Anniversary ed.). New York: Paulist Press.

Hughes, R., Ginnett, R., & Curphy, G. (2012). *Leadership: Enhansing the Lessons of Experience* (7th Edition ed.). New York: McGraw Hill Companies, Inc.

Pinnington, A. H. (2011). *Leadership Development: Applying the Same Leadership Theories and Development Practices to Different Contexts?* Leadership, 7(3), 335-365. doi: 10.1177/1742715011407388

Ross Sorkin, A. (2009). *Too Big To Fail.* New York: Penguin Group (USA) Inc.

van Dierendonck, D. (2011). "Servant Leadership: A Review and Synthesis." Journal of Management, 37(4), 1228-1261. doi: 10.1177/0149206310380462

Walumbwa, F., Avolio, B., Gardner, W., Wernsing, T., and Peterson, S. (2008). "Authentic Leadership: Development and Validation of a Theory-Based Measure?" *Journal of Management*, 34(1), 37. doi: 10.1177/0149206307308913

Section 3

Transformational Leadership

Karl Marx could be right. I am not saying he is, but I am saying that we must wait and see. Marx was a German philosopher during the 19th century who became famous for advocating communism. It was his position that the proletariat would rise up and overtake the bourgeoisie. This would imply that an empowered lower class, known in capitalistic terms as "blue-collar," would rise up and declare a new social order by taking over the upper class, known in capitalistic terms as "white-collar." I am not sure about the new social order framed by Marx, but I am convinced that today's followers, no matter the color of their collars, are restless at best and angered at worst at our current state of leadership.

Current leadership is not recognizing these more empowered followers who expose the less effective leader while demanding recognition for what they can bring to an organization. Their demand cries out not from a self-serving motive, but out of necessity in that the key to transformation is to include everyone in the decisions and processes associated with constant change. The transformational leader who is leading in a world of constant change not only hears these cries but invites them as an integral part of being effective.

This section is meant to help you become an effective transformational leader. I will ask you to again reflect on your purpose and values. As previously stated, you transform or change because you are adapting your behaviors and decisions toward a purpose guided by values. Being transformational includes building the capacity of yourself and others. Essential to this is creating a learning culture because, by nature, to transform is to learn. Optimal transformation will take place when learning includes everyone, leader and follower. And finally, transparency is inevitable given the untethered access everyone has to information.

Technology is transforming our world and has been principally responsible for the more empowered individual, to include the follower. Look at the ease anyone can access most any information. A prime example is the financial industry. For years financial firms have had proprietary information to make informed investment decisions or give informed advice. To access that information, you needed to be associated with that financial firm. Today that's not the case. I find myself "Googling" something most every day.

Similarly, it is easy to disseminate information on anyone whether that information is accurate or not. Facebook, Twitter, and LinkedIn are a few examples of how information is disseminated about most anything or anyone. Giving and getting untethered information at unprecedented speed that can be accessed by anyone, leader or follower, warrants quick responses that often require organizations to quickly change tactics or strategies in order to be competitive.

This is forcing us to look at transformation different than before. In today's fast-paced environment, change is constant in optimally efficient organizations; change is a normal process rather than an aberration to the status quo, thus implying that the status quo itself does not exist in optimally efficient organizations. Identifying what needs to be changed in a timely manner is now a matter of process. This process is less dependent on the intuitive leader and more dependent on a culture that encourages group think that invites input from all players, whether they be leaders or followers.

If identifying change is a process that involves everyone, followership development becomes something different than the power centric cultures of the past. Now everyone has responsibility for identifying needed change, not just leaders. This implies we must create a learning environment that builds the capacity of everyone and transforms the leader-follower relationship into a partnership approach rather than a vertical hierarchy.

Transformational leadership theory starts with an organization's culture, which is a function of a unifying purpose and a wholesome set of values, the subjects of Sections One and Two. The theory is then extended to the leader modeling behaviors that show a willingness to be transformed herself, connecting peers with purpose and values, building the capacity of the individual, creating a learning culture, and transparency.

21. Theory of Transformational Leadership

Culture: f(**purpose**; values)

Effective transformational leadership: f (**culture**; transforming yourself; connecting with purpose and values; building capacity; creating a learning culture; transparency)

To have stability in a world of change, something must stay constant. This is why purpose and values are so important to the transformational leader. When people have a common purpose and set of values to guide them, they can realize their potential to be transformational. This is done by pursuing strategies that lead to purpose and guided by values. While the strategies will change based on the ever-changing world, purpose and values provide a stability that guides decision making and standards of behavior. Merck's purpose of "ridding the world of disease" does not change, but the strategies and tactics for its realization are constantly reviewed and revised. *Being purpose based and values driven is essential to providing needed stability to a culture that recognizes change as a constant.*

Leaders negotiating environments that are constantly changing need to share responsibility, so everyone is inspired to recognize needed change and the strategies associated with change. That in itself is transformational for many leaders, for it changes how a leader thinks. As I write this section, the world is in the middle of a pandemic caused by the novel coronavirus. My prayer is that by the time you are reading this book, this crisis has passed, and we have some normalcy to our lives. However, I would guess that the fate of many organizations will rest with how quickly they identified needed change and its implementation while staying focused on a unifying purpose guided by group values.

Amid this pandemic, I recently had an extended conversation with Jerry, a pastor friend, who was wondering what church will look like in the future. Over the course of that conversation, many questions arose: How do you handle social distancing, disinfecting constantly, the use of masks, and so on? How do you collect offerings, give communion, or greet people as they arrive? How will people sit in church or how about church school for children and adults—what will that look like? How can you lead your church so that the practitioners feel safe to attend, thus allowing the church to realize its purpose?

Now, my friend Jerry is a very effective pastor, but he knows he does not have all the answers. Instead of resisting change, he embarked on a transformation process. Jerry identified people to form groups focused on exploring and discovering needed change. He did this so when the church physically reopened, the values and purpose remained steadfast, despite change being implemented. The transformation for Jerry started from "individual think" (he alone identifying needed change) to "group think" (inspiring others to take responsibility for identifying and implementing needed change).

For example, as a group it was decided to install a new air filtration system to help the congregation feel safer. Since physical attendance declined, the group decided to conduct two services instead of three, allowing more leadership involvement in the children's programs and adult Sunday School. Change became everyone's responsibility as it was everyone's responsibility to stay focused on the unifying purpose and be framed by a set of organizational values.

22. Transforming Yourself

Transformational Leadership: f (culture; **transforming yourself**; connecting with purpose and values; building capacity; creating a learning culture; transparency)

To understand transformation and transformational leadership, start by reflecting on how you led yourself during times of significant life changes. We have all been, to a lesser and greater degree, transforming most of our lives. We have, therefore, been constantly learning. Think for a moment. When in your life did you experience your biggest transformation? This would be a time of great change and great learning, and it was probably very difficult. Maybe it was when you left home for the first time. Maybe it was when you went to college, or maybe it was your first leadership position. Transformation may have been during a specific time of reinventing yourself. This reinvention often accompanies changing careers, forcing you to learn something totally new. Parents sometimes have to reinvent themselves after children leave home. Some of us have faced traumatic events such as divorce, the death of a spouse, or the death of a child, and we were forced to reinvent because of disruptions in the things most important to us.

These times forced change by putting you in a place that was unfamiliar. You were forced to cope with the change, and the coping forced you to learn. This learning is transformational. Change is a certainty, and to succeed during transformations, you must learn. As you emerged from these difficult times of uncertainty, upon reflection, what did you learn? How did you change? How were you transformed? Your answers should help inform you on how to lead others.

The respected leaders we reflected on at the beginning of the book were probably transformational leaders. What was it about these leaders that made them transformational? How were they effective at leading and managing change? The common answers I have heard in my many workshops include:

1. They communicated a unifying purpose and a set of core values.
2. They respected me, and I them.
3. They built my capacity by helping me realize my potential.
4. They understood that learning was important.
5. Their transparency served as a transformational leadership example.

Maybe you can learn some lessons about how to lead your followers by how these transformational leaders led you.

Make Yourself Vulnerable

On July 1, 1971, I hugged my mother, shook hands with my father, and walked towards the Sally Port of Washington Hall at the United States Military Academy at West Point. "Mister, drop your bags" was the first of many orders I received that day. It was given by "The Cadet in the Red Sash." He is infamous to those informed about West Point and that first day. I was ready for that first order because I was coached by a member of the West Point basketball team during the recruiting process. He advised me not to simply put my bag down but to physically drop it, because that was the order. I was ready for it. What I was not ready for, nor was the "Cadet in the Red Sash" who gave me the order, was my suitcase flying open, underwear and t-shirts tumbling out in the wind, and being blown across the area. "Mister, get your stuff now. Do you think I want to look at your stuff?! Get it now." I scrambled for my things. As I was running to retrieve my underwear blowing in the wind, I observed a tall new cadet, like me, laughing at the sight. Of course, several upperclassmen descended upon the new cadet for laughing. "Wipe that smirk off your face, Mister," I heard them say. He continued to smile, and they continued to yell. That new cadet's name, I would learn later, was Cornelius Gabriel Begley— "Neil" for short. He would become a lifelong buddy, a best friend.

Though I was ready to "drop my bag," I was not ready for most anything else. Our first day at West Point began our transformation to becoming military leaders, though it did not feel that way. We just wanted to survive. Neil and I had never met before this first day, but we had similar stories. In high school we were class presidents, all-state athletes, good students, and popular. But starting that day on July 1, we were nothing more than new cadets at West Point, no different than the other 1,500 who entered for the first time. We were vulnerable to starting something that we knew would be difficult, and we were afraid we may just not cut it. We were made to feel we knew nothing and had accomplished less. West Point made us vulnerable.

We learned how to do important things that day like eating

a square meal, folding socks, shining shoes, marching, and not smirking or laughing. Neil struggled with not smirking or laughing. I did not. Over the next four years and beyond, we were transformed from being broken down and feeling inadequate to developing a sense of confidence in knowing we could lead. Whether we realized it or not, we were made vulnerable to the pain of being *transformed.*

At West Point exists an intentional process to transform cadets to realize a purpose that focuses on service. This was a very personal transition physically, emotionally, and intellectually for all of us. Our lives were radically changed. To survive at West Point, we needed to cope with the change by openly learning and transforming. For those that survived the four-year experience (about half of us), we were intentionally transformed. More specifically, those who entered and stayed voluntarily chose a transformational experience that left us vulnerable and exposed. An entire community of instructors, administrators, and others were assembled with a purpose of inspiring learning.

This learning was more than the academic challenges associated with classroom instruction or homework. The other components of this transformation were more intrinsic. Learning socialization, accountability, and responsibility were among many dynamics that we developed outside the classroom. While some instances of learning seemed to have happened by accident—as part of the experience, others happened by design (like those lessons learned on day one).

I would challenge leaders to be intentional about what their constituents are learning. Through learning, people are transformed. We must create an environment that teaches and allows vulnerability. Colleges have a mission to inspire learning that will transform students to succeed in a particular field. Leaders have a responsibility to inspire learning that transforms constituents to fulfilling roles that contribute to realizing a purpose. Consider the leaders of Merck inspiring constituents to be transformed into roles that contribute to ridding the world of disease, or a church that inspires learning that transforms its constituents to making disciples of all people (Jesus's great commission).

West Point transforms cadets to become military officers that can negotiate change while focusing on a common purpose. Similarly, to realize your organization's purpose in a world of constant change, transformation must take place through learning. For yourself that may mean making yourself vulnerable by entering the unknown or unfamiliar. For others that allow themselves to take risk and be vulnerable, it may mean having leaders around them (like you) who contribute to their transformation.

When Life Throws You a Curve

Allowing yourself to be vulnerable is itself transformational. Unexpected events, though not voluntary, can force transformation. Traumatic events can transform a person. When life throws you a curve, you may be forced to change, like it or not. Examples of such events are divorce, death of a family member or close friend, loss of a job, or a severe financial set back. While negotiating these changes can be difficult, it can also give opportunity for great learning and transformation. These events can bring people into our lives that are true examples of transformational leaders and can serve as great examples for us to model our own behaviors after.

I challenge you to reflect on those times of great change and transformation in your life. For me, I think about the times when I had to vocationally reinvent myself. I remember leaving the Army after four years at West Point and twelve years on active duty. My military career was going great, and, for the most part, I enjoyed what I was doing. However, there was sickness in my family that I did not anticipate, and I was concerned about being deployed for long periods of time. I was caught by surprise as to the degree of learning and transformation I would need to succeed in the transition.

I interviewed for a security job only to discover the job was not for security at all; rather it was for selling securities. I had no financial experience whatsoever, which was exposed during the interview. My brother and his wife happened to be in the financial business, and after being coached by them, the interviewer agreed to interview me again, and I got the job. My name tag displayed my title of "trainee." This was a far cry from commanding soldiers in the Presidential Honor Guard, being Chief of Training for a division of over ten thousand soldiers or being a professor of military science. Transforming includes not only learning but may require a high dose of humility that can be uncomfortable. For me it was definitely uncomfortable. Fortunately, I had people around me that understood the challenges of the transition.

I met Peter, a senior financial advisor, who also had a military background. He appreciated the challenges associated with my transition. His friendship and support were critical to the painful transformation I was unexpectedly experiencing. Often Peter and I had intimate conversations about the financial industry and life in general. Peter was simply very generous with devoting time to my well-being. On the other hand, I had a manager, Barney, who did not understand learning and transformation. Barney did understand what was important to him and had little interest in my development and learning unless it served his self-serving purpose of position and making money.

His lack of understanding learning and transformation was very damaging to his followers, particularly me, the new guy, who needed to learn a new vocation. Barney was not trusted, and thus was not credible, and had little influence on his constituents. Over time I learned that his stagnant leadership style was consistent with the firm's inability to negotiate change and create a learning environment. Before the firm went out of business, I left and accepted a similar position with another financial firm. My departure was intentional.

Good leaders, like Peter, recognize vulnerability in followers and stand ready to help. Poor leaders also recognize this vulnerability and stand ready to take advantage for personal gain, like Barney, who benefited as a manager from my efforts without contributing to my success. Be a good leader. Over thirty years later, Peter is still one of my best friends.

Twenty years later, another forced transition took me by surprise: The unexpected death of my wife. My two daughters, Angela and Katie, ages 19 and 16 respectively, also were experiencing a difficult transition. I felt responsible for leading my family, along with leading a large division for a nationally branded financial firm. Soon after her death, it was apparent that I was not the only one experiencing stress. The financial industry was feeling pressure. Rob, my great coach and mentor I talked about earlier, was replaced (part of the transition that was going on in the financial industry as the 2008 financial crisis approached).

His replacement, Sue, was someone whom I had known and competed with for years. We approached our positions differently, which led to disagreement. After less than a year working under her, another forced transition. I was driving from Chattanooga, Tennessee to Ft. Worth, Texas to take Katy back to college to begin her sophomore year. In route, Sue called and asked me to pull over to the side of the road. Alongside the road, in my SUV packed with Katy's stuff, and with Katy in the passenger seat, I was informed that I was being forced to retire after nineteen years of employment with that company, effective immediately.

I continued the trip, returned, and went to work finding employment. To say I was in the midst of change is an understatement. The death of my wife, my youngest daughter leaving home, and now the loss of my job brought unexpected change into my life that was transformational.

Over the next several years I worked for several large and internationally known financial companies as a middle management executive. Like most leaders, I had a set of principles that guided my decisions and behaviors, like integrity, respecting others, and teamwork. However not having an intentional list of well-defined values to live by caused me to accept positions where my values were not appropriately aligned. I also found myself rationalizing decisions and behaviors that were not values driven as just part of a typical transition.

Despite this, I stayed true to some core principals. When I was encouraged to not tell the total truth (remember the compensation plan), terminate employees that did not deserve being terminated, intimidate employees towards focusing on objectives directly related to personal compensation in favor of the wholistic purpose, overlook obvious misconduct like forging signatures, and tolerate undeserved preferential treatment from upper-level management, I often decided not to conform.

How I handled this nonconformity was not often smooth or "politically correct." I could have done better trying to influence better decisions in others. Maybe I could have coached them or had a courageous and difficult conversation. Often, I did not. As I look back, it was clear that the advertised values of these organizations were not sincerely adopted by much of the leadership. It is also clear to me today that though my values were beginning to form, I was not clear in articulating or intentionally modeling the values that would define me.

I simply got tired of working in organizations whose senior leadership's values were so different from my yet-realized values. I wish I had read Section 2 of this book prior to accepting these positions. My values would have been discovered and defined. I could have been more intuitive in ensuring my values were appropriately aligned with the organizations and leaders I reported to.

However, times of transformation caused by unanticipated events can be as confusing as they are difficult. The death of my wife, being forced to leave my job, and the yet to be mentioned surprise death of my father all caught me off guard. Values give stability during unstable times. Conversely, unstable times can inspire a values discovery that is life changing. This happened to me, and I decided to take control.

I decided to move away from an industry I had worked in for many years. I left the financial industry and my home in Florida in favor of being more intentional about taking control of my transforming life. I got up for the first time in my adult life with nothing to do.

One of the people who stepped forward to lead me during these transitional (and difficult) times was Jerry. Jerry was the senior pastor I spoke of earlier of a large Seventh Day Adventist church near my home. He had attended Andrews University years before and had familiarity with their leadership program. Jerry suggested I check out Andrews University's leadership program and consider applying for their PhD program.

Coincidently, Senator Bob Corker of Tennessee (then the mayor of Chattanooga) encouraged me to help develop business leaders in Chattanooga, where I live. I have lived my life taking risks with my future. The decisions to go to West Point, attending the US Army Ranger program, leaving the financial industry at the height of my career, all were made in a very naïve, yet optimistic context. This was just one more risk. My risk-taking efforts of the past were very transformational, yet rewarding and successful.

So why not? At Jerry's prodding I went back to college at age 58. After five years, I received a Doctor of Philosophy degree in leadership and have spent my time since writing, speaking, teaching, and living a life focused on improving leadership in our communities.

As I look back on these unintended transformational times, I often ask myself what got me through. Courage and tenacity were important. However, Peter, Rob, Jerry, and others inspired me to have that courage and tenacity. Their examples informed my belief that being vulnerable can build my capacity, embrace transparency, and inspire my learning. The result was my being successful at negotiating change. Their examples helped me establish my purpose and frame my values, providing the needed stability during unstable times. *My wish for you is for you to be intentional about modeling behaviors needed by someone you lead during times of transformation.*

Upon reflection, I learned that effective transformational leadership means staying connected to purpose and values, building the capacity of others, always be learning, and the importance of transparency.

23. Connecting with Purpose and Values

Where Is Stability in the Midst of Change?

Sections 1 and 2 are based on the theory that a unifying purpose guided by values defines the culture of an organization. This foundation becomes even more important for the transformational leader and deserves even more consideration.

Transforming Means Connecting with Purpose

Having an overarching purpose unifies efforts, making everyone an agent of change. This unifying spirit keeps everyone on the team changing as the environment dictates, according to realizing the purpose. The purpose is the anchor that keeps needed change relevant and makes change everyone's responsibility. People do not make transformational change because they are ordered to. Ordered change may work in the short term, but changes that transform are inspired from within, focused on a wholesome purpose.

Hence, the importance of a purpose inspires collective efforts.

Without a unifying purpose, change is splintered and motivated by principally selfish intents. With a unifying purpose, short-term and self-serving goals such as personal recognition, money, or promotion, are healthy and needed as the group realizes its selfless purpose while these goals are accomplished.

Stated differently, let's compare purposes that are "finite" as opposed to purposes that are "infinite." Having a purpose of building the best mainframe computer, as IBM did, is finite since mainframe computers became obsolete. In Section 1, I described the drug company Merck as having a purpose of ridding the world of disease. This purpose is infinite because I cannot picture a world without disease. The Turkish Monk's egg business had finite business goals, but their purpose was infinite, to continually teach and encourage Christian practices in the business community.

This is not meant to undermine the importance of finite goals. However, we must always guard against goals receiving such importance that they become misconstrued as the purpose. *Established goals are for the benefit of realizing the overarching purpose. Transformational leaders must always be reminders of that connection.* Purpose is infinite and is something that everyone can focus on indefinitely into the future. Goals are finite and are established for the benefit of realizing purpose.

Connecting peers with purpose framed by values engages peers in purposeful interaction where learning is accelerated and needed change is more fully discovered. When everyone is connected to purpose and framed by values, the ideas that generate change come from group think and are products of group learning. The ideas of change come from within, through dialogue and expression. The leader simply must keep this momentum of dialogue and thinking going in the context of realizing the unified purpose.

Leadership is not experienced from top down or even from

bottom up. It is a collective effort focused on the overarching purpose governed by values. Teamwork is a natural product of this collective effort and creates an environment that is more effective in solving complex problems. *A critical leadership function is to consistently remind the team of the unifying purpose and continually inspire dialogue and thinking towards its realization.*

Transforming Means Connecting with Values

Leadership development at West Point focuses on the growth of the cadet's intellect, military competence, physical advancement, and character. Though character development was always important, only recently was a systematic character development strategy created. The new strategy, named *Live Honorably and Build Trust,* starts the first day a young man or woman enters West Point. Living honorably is the internalization of West Point's values of Duty, Honor, Country, as well as the Army's values of Loyalty, Duty, Respect, Selfless Service, Honor, Integrity, and Personal Courage.

This development or internalization does not happen overnight. Cadets, much like new employees or new members of a team, enter with their own set of values shaped by friends, family, communities, and experiences. These values may not be aligned with the values of the organization. However, from the moment cadets arrive on campus, an intentional effort is made to begin the transformation towards West Point's values. They are taught by cadet cadre, staff, faculty, and the entire West Point community, all of whom are expected to serve as role models. Cadets are led to view right and wrong through the prism of West Point values. They are guided in reflection and introspection, engaged in open dialogue using peer led small group forums, and coached in making decisions and guiding behavior based on values.

Through this approach, they are inspired to internalize West Point's and the Army's values, and with that they "Live Honorably" with all that implies. They are transformed.

It seems to reason that any reputable organization would have embedded values that inspire leaders to intentionally develop strategies to transform participants towards their adoption. Section 2 provides a 'how to' guide for getting started, however this takes time, but the character of organizations depends on the success of this transformational effort. People do not naturally transform themselves toward a wholesome purpose framed by values. They must be led there.

A powerful part of this transformation is found in role models. Role models serve as an inspirational and powerful example of how to behave and make decisions according to a set of group values that inform transformation. Role models impacted my transformation at West Point and beyond. I was impacted by the selfless service of a professor visiting me in the hospital when I had mononucleosis, to teach me the day's lesson; a German professor who would go out of his way to tell me how well I was "coming along;" or a loyal classmate and great friend who stayed up with me until the early hours of the morning drilling me on the next day's history exam so I would not fail; and the courage of an officer being critical of my behavior with the sole intent of bringing me to a standard of excellence so I could understand my potential. All these role models lived the values of the organization. These leaders changed me forever; they were transformational leaders and they served as an example of the kind of leader I wanted to become.

Changing Values

Donna is the CEO of a nonprofit agency located in Chattanooga, Tennessee. After taking over, she soon discovered that the values embedded among some of the leadership team were not aligned with her values or the values needed to successfully move the organization into the future. She began to transform the organization... first by intentionally instructing, modeling, and behaving according to her personal set of values. This was followed by instituting values workshops for the management team that discovered and advertised their personal values, explored what values currently represented the group, then decided what values would be needed for a successful future.

As a matter of practice, she recognized employees who displayed behaviors aligned with the values, consistently highlighted certain values at every opportunity, and coached her direct reports according to these values. Some leaders left, being replaced by leaders with personal values that were more closely aligned with the group's values. It has taken several years, but the entire organization has transformed.

I have often been asked, "How often does an organization need to review and possibly change its values?" My answer is when morale is bad, where behaviors are bad, or where poor decisions are rationalized away as being okay. It is then time to resurrect values and be transformed.

However, it must start with leaders who can serve as role models. These leaders have discovered their personal values and live them. Their values are mostly aligned with the organization's values. With that base, other role models will follow. The local 911 communication center in Tennessee transformed its culture by framing a set of values that represented the organization, discovered alignment between personal and organizational values among the principal leaders, and then hired, fired, coached, behaved, made decisions, and taught its leaders according to these values and how they were defined.

Their process for discovering and defining values was described in Section 2. From their efforts, role models emerged who modeled values-driven decisions and behaviors. People were hired and promoted, coached out, and replaced. Over time, the organization was transformed.

I challenge you to reflect on those leaders you most respected and how they represented the organization's values through their decisions and behaviors. Note how they recognized good decisions and behaviors as they related to the values and how they responded to inappropriate behaviors and decisions that are not aligned. Be like them. Then be intentional through training, coaching, and living according to those values. It will take time, but your organization will transform its culture to be values driven, and you will be a transformational leader.

24. Building Capacity

Effective transformational leadership: f (culture; transforming yourself; connecting with purpose and values; **building capacity**; creating a learning culture; transparency)

I was walking into the cafeteria of Southfield Village Elementary School in Monroe, Michigan. I was in 4th grade and looking forward to lunch and recess afterward. It had been a tough morning. I had arrived late and was yelled at for something I cannot remember. I opened up my brown bag that my mother so carefully packed. A bologna sandwich, small bag of carrots, and a container of apple sauce; it was going to be great. As I bit into my sandwich, I felt a sharp pain ripping through my neck into my head. All I could see was black. I spit out my sandwich. I painfully turned around as Mrs. Schultz was bending over me yelling at me again. Apparently, she struck me in the back of the neck causing me to see black. I don't remember what I had done wrong that prompted my punishment, but I will never forget Mrs. Schultz.

There were three classes of 4th graders; one for the smart, one for the average, and one for the dumb kids—as we referred to them and us. Mrs. Schultz taught the 'average' kids. I spent most of my efforts trying to stay out of trouble. The mischief in me made that difficult. She gave me a 'D' in citizenship. I probably deserved it. I remember Debbie, whom I did not like, got a third place in the science fair for her bird display. I thought her display was stupid, and I snuck her ribbon from her exhibit and placed it on mine — a bowl of plants my mother actually planted. Not very good citizenship on my part; hence my 'D.'

I have no recollection of learning anything in fourth grade. My academic performance mirrored my citizenship performance. I was glad to move on to Mrs. Carney's 5th grade class. Mrs. Carney also taught the 'average' kids. I loved Mrs. Carney. For art, I drew a picture of the Seal of the United States of America that she said was so good it would be used in our class play. She let me play George Washington in the play. At the end of the year, she even gave me the Citizenship Award and presented it to me in front of the class with my mother present.

I learned to take pride in my work and myself. I learned a lot in 5th grade. I was very proud of receiving that award, the seal I drew, being in the play, and actually receiving good grades. For 6th grade, Mrs. Carney recommended me for Mrs. Everett's class. Mrs. Everett taught the "smart" kids. That changed my life. It was like getting a promotion. For the first time I thought of myself as being maybe better than average. Mrs. Carney not only believed in me, but she **inspired me to believe in myself**.

Judgment Versus Judgementalism

As I reflected on my relationships with my 4th and 5th grade teachers, it is evident that there were great differences between the two. Mrs. Schultz was also my older brother's 4th grade teacher two years before me. David was not a "good student" and struggled academically. That struggle would continue throughout 5th grade, where Mrs. Carney was also his teacher. As I reflect back, it appears that Mrs. Schultz expected nothing more from me than she got from my brother David. That was judgmental. Mrs. Schultz was two years from retirement. Again, upon reflection, her priority was most likely to survive those last two years, putting the development of her students second behind her survival. She cared little about me.

Mrs. Carney, on the other hand, looked at me as a valued person in her class who deserved the right to be taught without being impacted by any preconceived notions of the teacher. She was concerned with me and my future. A selfless motive within her inspired her to judge me fairly and accurately and help me be better. That judgment was no different than any leader who assesses the skill of a follower and creates a developmental plan focused on that individual (in this case a child), independent of self-sacrifice.

Without her I would have continued thinking of myself as just another average kid maybe indefinitely, with no special talents or skills.

This is worth deep reflection from all leaders. Building capacity involves inspiring our followers to have the competence and self-confidence to be transformed themselves. Being judgmental prevents that from happening. *Creating capacity is all about inspiring people to believe in themselves and has little room for judging others due to things out of their control such as skin color, sex, weight, tattoos, family, or anything beyond their control.*

Transformational Versus Transactional

In Section 2, I told the story about the developing of a financial planning strategy of two financial firms. One firm inspired financial planning by rewarding those who did financial planning and punishing those who did not embrace the strategy. The primary objective of many was focused on self, or what one could get. "If I do this, I get that." It was a transaction. In the other firm, where I led a region years later, we motivated financial advisors through education. We funded their Certified Financial Planner designation. Through that education, knowledge was acquired that could help them serve their clients better. It was transformational.

I do not want to imply that giving rewards and recognition is wrong, in fact, I believe just the opposite. If someone does well, I want them to be promoted to another level, even in the early stages of a career where the principal motivation may be to get that promotion—a transaction that has a self-serving flavor to it. But as one gets more experienced and learns more, a transition needs to occur where the leader's primary motivation is inspired by the overriding wholesome purpose guided by values rather than personal gain.

Today's leaders that hope to move forward in their professions to higher levels must be less focused on the transaction (what they get), like Mrs. Schulz or Frank, from Section 2, or probably the leader you did not admire, in favor of being more focused on transformation (what they can give), like Mrs. Carney, Rob from Section 2, or probably the leader you admired.

For some, this transition never happens. For others it does, and these should be the candidates for positions of increased responsibility. So, the question becomes, "How can we be more intentional about developing transformational leaders rather than transactional leaders?" One strategy involves developing a learning culture.

25. Developing a Learning Culture

Effective transformational leadership: f (culture; transforming yourself; connecting with purpose and values; building capacity; **developing a learning culture**; transparency)

Transformational leaders effectively lead in environments that are in a constant state of flux. New business models, new technologies emerging, and evolving market behaviors are evolving at an ever-increasing pace. The ability to learn fast has become important to compete and be successful. Today's leaders must resist pontificating how it has always been done in the past in favor of experimenting with new things and pushing yourself to expand your capabilities while still performing your job. It may be uncomfortable to experiment with new things, and, in some cases, experienced people will feel like beginners as they, and you, learn and change. However, effective transformational leaders create learning cultures that can overcome these fears. Developing a learning culture must include three intentional strategies: preparing yourself to learn, preparing and inspiring your followers to learn, and inspiring team learning.

Preparing Yourself to Learn

Be aspirational. Leading by example is an important leadership trait. If a leader wants an organization of learners, then the leader's approach to learning is important. A leader's embrace of self-development inspires others to self-develop. If you notice comments towards learning like "it will take too long," "we have always done it this way," or "here we go again with another flash in the pan," you may have a problem. Leaders who focus on the negative reinforce a lack of aspiration to learning. *It is essential that leaders prepare to learn by genuinely aspiring to learn themselves.*

I recently conducted a values-based leadership workshop for the newly appointed sergeants of a city's police department. The intent of the workshop was to inspire participants to make decisions and behave according to a personal set of values that were hopefully aligned with the department's values. This four-hour workshop would satisfy a state mandate of having the new sergeants attend leadership training.

Early in the four-hour session, it became clear that most of the participants did not want to be there, were not familiar with the current department's values, and were there for one reason—to get the four hours of mandatory training. After the workshop, I had conversations with many of the lieutenants and captains that the sergeants reported to. I was disappointed to learn that the lieutenants and captains had little interest in the content of the workshop, did not care if learning took place, and had little interest in learning themselves. What an opportunity lost!

I conducted the same workshop with the local 911 communications center mentioned earlier. I never realized the technical expertise, training, and leadership structure needed in organizing three shifts, managing time off, meals, discipline, security, and so much more. This effort, unlike the local city police department, started with training the executive director and his direct reports. We then systematically moved down the chain-of-command with the same training. There were challenges, but it was clear that everyone was expected to learn, be open to new ideas, and be developed. Learning began with the principal leaders modeling what it means to be an aspirational learner. Soon their example was modeled by others, and the creation of a learning culture got traction.

Be self-aware. Being self-aware is not an unfamiliar concept. Leaders have grown accustomed to getting feedback and recognizing how others see them. However, assessing what you need to learn can be very inaccurate. What we know versus what we do not know, skills we have versus skills we do not have but need, or an openness to expanding our own knowledge into areas we fall short, are important parts to a leader wanting to learn.

I have found that most leaders who assess themselves accurately are intentional about examining their biases and striving for greater objectivity and are thus open to others' opinions. The self-awareness of the executive director of the 911 communication center was evident in that he was an active participant in every workshop, wanting to learn and be developed himself. He was an excellent listener. His active listening and desire to learn flowed over to the other leaders.

Be a curious leader. Curious leaders are like children with an urge to learn and master new things. A curious leader is willing to walk a path even if she is not sure where it may lead. The executive director of the 911 communications center did not know where our values discovery workshop would take him or his organization. However, he was curious to find out. The city police department's curiosity was primarily wondering what they were having for lunch when the four required hours were complete. Their objective was to get the four hours completed with no curiosity as to what can be learned or what things could change for the better.

Like many of you, your first several years in college may have been difficult. For me it was. Academics were particularly challenging. At West Point, we were graded on a 3.0 scale with 2.0 being passing. We called that being "tangent." If I got a score on a quiz of 2.1, I had one tenth in the bank. Exams may be worth six, nine, or even twelve or more units. On a test worth 12 units, a score of 8.0 was "tangent." If I received a score of 9.1 on the exam, I banked eleven "tenths." If I received a score of 7.0, I lost ten "tenths." My objective in every class was to score at tangent-level or better. Doing so meant I survived. Learning was secondary.

My principal survival technique was memorization. This technique took twice as long, but I thought was key to survival. I had no curiosity to learn. I just wanted to survive, which I did — barely. The last two years I began to understand that the real key to not only survival, but accomplishment, was to learn and be curious about the subject. The subject of thermodynamics is understandable if you appreciate the basics as to how fluid flows around an object. Or mechanical engineering is better understood if you set back and logically appreciate and are curious as to why something performs the way it does given weight, friction, size, and other variables. I became curious as to the "why" things were, and I learned. Ironically the more I focused on learning (and less on grades) my grades improved dramatically.

Our followers need to know "why" things are to satisfy, or maybe develop, their curiosity. With that knowledge they will be better able to succeed in a constantly changing environment. When that curiosity to learn is exemplified by the leader, they are preparing and inspiring their followers to do the same.

Preparing and Inspiring Your Followers to Learn

Be vulnerable. One of the differences between the leader you respected versus the one you did not was probably self-confidence. A self-confident leader will sometimes risk trying new things even if there is a chance that the experiment turns out to be wrong. Experimenting with change will sometimes make things better and sometimes not, but you do not know until you try. The confident leader is ready to admit and take responsibility for a mistake. This confidence models the accepting of mistakes as a part of learning. A leader who looks at his mistakes and the mistakes made by others as learning opportunities inspires learning.

Have you ever taken a foreign language? The class probably required speaking aloud. Speaking aloud advertises weakness in speaking the language but informs the instructor on struggles in learning. For me, the more I spoke in class, even at the risk of getting a lower grade, the more I learned.

Secure leaders who allow themselves to be vulnerable are examples of being learners themselves. Those leaders allow followers the freedom to take appropriate risk and learn. Great opportunities to learn are imbedded in our mistakes. Be vulnerable to making mistakes and do not avoid owning up to the mistakes. Expect the same from your followers. There are no excuses when mistakes are made, but when one takes responsibility for a mistake, learning takes place.

Remember me failing that commodity registration exam at

about the same time Marge failed her principal exam? It was the story I told in Section One where I was advised to fire my chief operations officer, Marge. One of Marge's challenges was being perceived as incompetent. This was exemplified by her failing to pass the principal's exam. At the same time Marge was taking the principal exam, I was to take the commodity exam. We both failed on this first attempt. I immediately informed the leadership team of my failure (exposing vulnerability) and informed the team as to how I would prepare for taking the exam a second time. Marge, unlike previous failed attempts where she did not immediately try to retake the exam, developed a similar plan for taking her exam again. If I was going to take a failure and turn it into a success, so was she. She followed my example. We both passed the second time and I hope we both learned something about ourselves. To prepare and inspire followers to learn, the leader must model learning behaviors, even if that means admitting mistakes or failure and then learning from them.

The transformational leader inspires a culture of learning. This includes individual and group learning. This is what makes the environment current, creative, and challenging. Change naturally evolves in environments that are constantly learning. The leader is not saddled with ideas of change; rather the culture that is constantly learning accepts that responsibility. How is such an environment created? There are two critical aspects to a learning environment. The first aspect involves team learning, while the second aspect involves conflict resolution.

Inspire Team Learning

I was in a meeting with twelve of my peers. Collectively, we represented the principal leaders for much of the country's largest brokerage firm. Each year the firm had a campaign usually lasting four months that focused on tactical objectives like opening new accounts, completing financial plans, or increasing retirement plans under management. The twelve of us were to brainstorm ideas how to successfully negotiate this year's campaign. On the surface, we were there to learn from one another; in reality, we were in direct competition.

During this meeting, learning was secondary, second to see who could come up with the best idea. Success meant someone admitting in front of everyone that someone else had the best idea. A discussion ensued. This particular year I did have the best idea — a system of advertising accountability that would publicly report results daily. We all adapted the idea, and I was congratulated. I won. We all went back to our respective regions to implement the idea.

As I reflect, I came to some conclusions. First, I am not convinced that there were not better ideas. My idea had been used before and lacked creativity for something new and maybe more current. Second, I suspect some participants were 'holding back' their ideas (for whatever reason) so we may not have had the benefit of collaboration that could surface the best ideas. People learned little in these kinds of meetings. There was more interest in talking rather than listening.

Upon returning to my headquarters, I got all my managers together to put in place the best plan to successfully negotiate this challenge. There were eleven of us. This meeting was very different than the previous discussion. Rather, a dialogue ensued. That meant everyone was engaged with the collective purpose of learning from each other so we as a group could succeed. The effort was focused on group success rather than individual success. That did not mean that the individual talents of each individual manager were not showcased. Individual talents were put on display, respected, and applied to winning.

Joe was exceptionally knowledgeable in financial planning and openly shared his ideas. Similarly, Jason and Jim had been very successful in creating a business focused on professional money management. They shared and discussed their ideas, and a dialogue ensued. Rusty was the most seasoned manager of the group and reminded us that this was less about winning a contest and more about realizing our overarching purpose of helping each client accomplish their financial goals. That put in context the transactional aspects of awards and winning in favor of a more transformational dynamic of doing the best thing for those we serve. Through doing so, we would be realizing our wholesome purpose.

At the conclusion of the meeting, we had a plan, but it did not stop there. Managers began calling their peers to brainstorm ideas, get advice, and encourage each other. That year our region was ranked the best. We all won! But more importantly, we all taught each other and learned from each other. It was dialogue that inspired the best ideas and made the difference.

In Peter Senge's 2006 book entitled, *The Fifth Dimension: The Art and Practice of Learning Organizations*, in his chapter on team learning, he states:

> The discipline of team learning involves the mastering the practices of dialogue and discussion, the two distinct ways teams converse. In dialogue, there is a free and creative exploration of complex and subtle issues, a deep "listening" to one another and suspending on one's own views. (p. 237)

In a world of a more empowered follower, the ideas captured in dialoguing bring into focus a recognition that everyone has equal value. It is through the "deep listening" to one another that we truly achieve dialogue. It replaces the need to "win," consistent with the culture of a discussion, with a collective effort of ideas and solutions that can only be accessed through the whole of the group, consistent with the culture of a dialogue. People do not compete but participate, separating themselves from their thought and thus become more creative, receptive, and productive. The sum of the individual's contributions equates to something much greater and allows for a discovery of something new and, hopefully, better.

There are three basic conditions that are necessary for a dialogue:

1. All participants must "suspend" their assumptions.
2. All participants must regard one another as colleagues.
3. There must be a facilitator who holds the context of the dialogue.

This takes practice and coaching, for it is difficult for many leaders to accept followers as colleagues where their views are essential to great learning. However, it is important to support a culture where opinions are honestly expressed, thus stretching the imaginations of all participants.

Resolving Conflict—The Four Seasons Hotels and Resorts.

The key to learning and transformational leadership is resolving conflict in a healthy and positive way. Conflict can present an opportunity to learn and be transformed, which is often missed. Leaders who can resolve conflict through improved learning have an edge on creating cultures conducive to healthy change. In Roger Martin's 2009 book, *The Opposable Mind*, the author argues two opposing views can lead to a third view that is better than those in opposition. This was the case with the Four Seasons Hotel and Resorts.

Isadore Sharp is the founder of what is today known as the Four Seasons Hotels and Resorts. Sharp, after graduating from college, joined the family construction business. While he was building a hotel for a client, he decided to build and run his own hotel. He struggled to find funding, but after six years he finally had the money for the project. Outside of Toronto, he built a small 125-room hotel, and thus was born the Four Seasons Hotel. During this time there were two kinds of hotels. One kind was a small motel, located outside of town, with usually fewer than two hundred rooms, with modest amenities providing not much more than a television in each room, an ice maker down the hall, and maybe a small bar or restaurant. This warm and intimate atmosphere with good service was fitting for a family on a budget and was less expensive to build.

The alternative hotel was located downtown and catered to the business traveler. This hotel was more expensive to build because of location, had more rooms, and offered expanded amenities such as conference facilities, multiple restaurants, banquet rooms, and workout facilities. Sharp loved his cozy Four Seasons Hotel, and built several of them, but it did not satisfy the needs of the business traveler. His fourth hotel was a sixteen hundred-room downtown convention center that also became profitable.

At this critical juncture, disagreement arose among the management team as to where the hotel needed to focus, the corporate guest or the family guest, as both guests wanted different things. Corporate guests needed meeting rooms, banquet style food service, and workout facilities, while family guests wanted a more intimate setting to include swimming pools plus restaurants where families could enjoy a private meal together.

Sharp got his management team together and presented these different views as an opportunity to come up with a third view that would satisfy all concerns. After much debate, listening, and learning, the Four Seasons Hotel and Resort was born. Team learning means we come together, not stay apart, to resolve conflict and learn as a group. It means we may disagree, but we still respect each other as valued members of the team focused on a unifying purpose.

They concluded their dialogue with an agreed-upon purpose:

> We have chosen to specialize within the hospitality industry by offering only experiences of exceptional quality. Our objective is to be recognized as the company that manages the finest hotels, resorts, and residence clubs wherever we locate. We create properties of enduring value using superior design and finishes and support them with a deeply instilled ethic of personal service. Doing so allows Four Seasons to satisfy the needs and tastes of our discerning customers, and to maintain our position as the world's premier luxury hospitality company.

Resolving the conflict between the two models produced the privately-held Four Seasons Hotels and Resorts that evolved into one of the great brands and organizations in the hospitality industry, with luxury hotels and resorts worldwide.

I would challenge leaders when facing conflict to keep asking questions that are focused on the over-arching purpose while keeping the corporate values thoroughly intact, maybe referring to them often. Secondly, avoid being clouded with emotion or even your own opinion. Remember, in dialogue we must suspend personal opinions and listen intently. Finally, emphasize listening. The listening reveals learning that evokes change.

26. Transparency

Effective transformational leadership: f (culture; transforming yourself; connecting with purpose and values; building capacity; creating a learning culture; **transparency**)

Recall the meeting with the eleven managers from the last chapter (team learning). where we had a dialogue that transformed the operation. Well, what I have shared about that meeting is not the entire story. One of the managers, let's call her Liz, sat quietly, seemed to be listening intently, but contributed little to the dialogue. Liz was an experienced manager with special expertise in compliance; however, she was new to this group. Yet she had a good feel for the administrative and operational side of the business. I felt her intuition was important.

At the end of the morning, I pulled her aside and asked what she thought of the dialogue so far. She said she thought it was good but that the subjects did not fall in her area of expertise and that she was uncomfortable making suggestions. I reminded Liz of her two decades of experience and how valuable her thoughts could be, regardless of whether the discussion involved her direct areas of responsibility. She reiterated she was uncomfortable sharing her honest thoughts with the group.

Usually when we talk about transparency, we appropriately are referring to leaders being transparent to followers. I have experienced times when I wondered if we were getting the whole story or just part of it? I argue that transparency applies to everyone, leader and follower. It is an integrity issue when we are hearing only a part of the story rather than the full story from those we report to. Similarly, is it an integrity issue when someone does not contribute or share knowledge that may help the group realize its over-arching purpose?

Did Liz violate our value of integrity by not contributing when she could have? Transparency takes on a different meaning when someone *could* contribute but does not because of insecurities or feelings that they would not be listened to. Transparency applies to everyone, and in this instance, Liz could have been more transparent.

I am not sure why Liz did not contribute to the dialogue during the morning session. Maybe because she was reasonably new to this group and felt like she needed to get to know the people better before contributing. Maybe because she was one of the few women in a group dominated by men. Maybe she felt unqualified to be there and was intimidated. Or maybe she did not trust me and was concerned that her comments would be judged, negatively, impacting her career.

I am not sure; nonetheless, I believe she was not transparent and that her unwillingness to share could stem from an integrity issue. She was more into the discussion mode rather than the dialogue mode. However, I felt responsible for her not feeling safe enough to contribute to the dialogue. Her not contributing hurt us from having a transformational culture that was constantly learning from each other. I had to do something.

Over lunch I sat with Liz and two other managers. I asked Liz specifically what she thought of Rusty's comment about making sure we keep the best interest of the client front and center while also accomplishing our strategic objectives. She answered that she thought that was important. I then asked her, given her compliance experience, how we would do that. She thought a greater effort to support financial advisors in the financial planning efforts through education and resources would inspire these advisors to switch their focus on how they could serve their clients (transformational) rather than what they could get themselves through financial planning (transactional).

That afternoon the dialogue shifted, and Liz was clearly engaged. We decided to hire an insurance specialist and an estate planning attorney to educate and support the financial advisors. A brilliant outcome developed that worked well in the long run, and this outcome would not have happened without Liz.

Creating a safe environment where everyone is totally transparent and engaged in dialogue is the transformational leader's responsibility. Thus leaders need to inspire dialogue where inclusion and team solutions are emphasized and the team wins, rather than discussions where individuals compete for the best idea while subordinating team solutions and individual victories are the priority. Today's leaders are partnering with members of their team to inspire dialogue. This leads to learning, which leads to discovering and adjusting to constant change, which leads to transformation.

27. Concluding Thoughts

Concluding Thoughts on Transformational Leadership and Action Steps

This section introduced a theory on becoming an effective transformational leader. This theory includes the importance of values and purpose in creating the best culture to transform. It argues that transformational leaders lead by example, that they allow themselves to be transformed, that discovering and implementing appropriate change is a group effort, and that it is important to connect every individual with the organization's purpose and values. It further posits that building capacity in each individual gives every team member the confidence to contribute, creating a transparent learning culture where everyone has the freedom and courage to express their views.

I believe there is one major skill that every leader must have to be successful. I feel this skill is so essential for learning, so I have reserved an entire section to its calling. Look at the leaders you respected. I am sure he or she was an excellent coach. This is the subject of Section 4.

Action Steps

I. When everything is finished, what do you want to accomplish, personally and professionally?
1. What is your personal purpose?
2. What is the purpose of your organization?
3. How do the organizations you are affiliated with contribute to you realizing your personal purpose?

II. Today, what are the goals over the next year of your organization?
1. How do these goals, when achieved, contribute to your organization realizing its purpose?
2. How do these goals, when realized, contribute to your personal purpose?
3. Once accomplished, how will you be rewarded? Explain in both transactional and transformational terms.

III. What are the values of your organization?
1. How do these values inform your decisions and behaviors in your efforts to accomplish these goals?
2. In the past in your organization' quest to accomplish short or intermediate goals, how have values played or not played into decisions and behaviors.

IV. Does an environment exist where everyone cares and respects everyone… leader, follower, and coworker?
1. Grade your organization, A thru F, on how well people respect each other
2. What needs to happen for a higher grade?

3. What can you personally commit to doing to raise the grade?

V. What was your last mistake?
   1. How did you deal with it? Now looking back, what would you change in how you dealt with it?
   1. What did you learn?

VI. Recall a mistake that someone who reported to you made.
   1. How did they deal with it?
   2. How did you deal with it?
   3. What did you learn?

VII. Describe a real complex problem your organization is or will be dealing with?
   1. What is the process for discovering its solution?
   2. Would you consider the problem being communicated in a transparent way?
   3. How could collaboration be instituted to discover a solution? Or how is the follower included in finding a solution or even identifying needed change to solve the problem?

VIII. Consider the following quote: Humility comes from a deep recognition of my limitations, faults, and internal struggles, but not at the expense of recognizing my gifts, abilities, and positive qualities. Humility is a joyful embrace of humanity—no more, no less.
   1. So, what are your limitations, faults, internal struggles?
   2. What are your gifts, abilities, and positive traits?
   3. How does reflecting on these and advertising them help you be a better leader?

4. How do you allow followers to conduct a similar journey safely?

IX. Does your organization have a learning culture or environment?
1. Does the organization use 'discussion' (there is a winner and a loser) or does the organization use 'dialogue' (everyone is a winner)?
2. How does your organization support a learning culture when resolving conflict?
3. How should your organization resolve conflict?
4. What can you personally do to support a learning culture?
5. What can you do differently to bring a system of learning into your organization that includes everyone?

X. What skills would you like to be more intentional about developing within yourself?
1. What are you going to do personally to develop those skills?
2. What support do you need from your organization to develop those skills?

XI. What can we do differently to bring a system of learning into your organization that includes everyone?

XII. Reflect on this section on transformation and discussions that ensued. What is your advice to your organization? What are you going to do differently based on what you have learned from this section and its action steps?

Contributing Work
to Section 3

This work helped inspire some
of the key concepts

1. Cooper, T. D. (2006). *Making Judgments without Being Judgmental.* Madison, WI: InterVarsity Press.

2. Cummings, T., & Worley, C. (Eds.). (2009). *Organizational Development and Change* (Ninth ed.). Mason, OH: South-Western Cengage Learning.

3. Drucker, P. (1999). "Managing Oneself." *Harvard Business Review,* 13.

4. Fullan, M. (2008). *The Six Secrets of Change.* San Fransisco: Josse-Bass.

5. Gupta, P. (2011). "Leading innovation change—The Kotter Way. *International journal of Innovation Science, 3*(3), 9.

6. Kellerman, B. (2012). *The End of Leadership* (First ed.). New York: Harper Collins Publishers.

7. Kotter, J. P. (1990). "What Leaders Really Do." *Harvard Business Review, 68*(3), 103-111.

8. Martin. (2007). *The Opposable Mind: How Successful Leaders Win through Integrative Thinking.* Boston, MA: Harvard Business School.

9. Martin, & Roger. (2009). *The Opposable Mind : Winning Through Integrative Thinking.* Boston: Harvard Business Rview.

10. Rosenzweig, P. (2007). *The Halo Effect.* New York: Free Press.

11. Senge, P. (2006). *The Fifth Dimension: The Art and Practice of Learning Organizations.* New York: Doubleday.

12. Smith, W. (December 6, 2008). Speech by Win Smith (as in Merrill Lynch Pierce Fenner and Smith). Paper presented at the Merrill Lynch Annual Meeting to Stockholders, Princeton, NJ.

13. Stevenson, L., & Haberman, D. (2009). *The Ten Theories of Human Nature* (5th ed.). New York: Oxford University Press.

14. Stragalas. (2010). "Improving Change Implementation: Practical Adaptions of Kotter's Model." *ODpractitioner, 42*(1), 9.

15. Turak, A. (2012). *The Trappist Way: Business Wisdom of the Trappist Monk.* Columbia University. Columbia, SC.

16. Harms, P., & Crede, M. (2010). "Emotional Intelligence and Transformation and Transactional Leadership: A Meta-Analysis." *Journal of Leadership & Organizational Studies, 17*(5), 12. doi: 10.1177/1548051809350894

17. Hughes, R., Ginnett, R., & Curphy, G. (2012). *Leadership: Enhancing the Lessons of Experience* (7th Edition ed.). New York: Mc-Graw Hill Companies, Inc.

Section 4

Coaching

Effective Effort: f(**A leader's coaching** + A motivated constituent)

**Effort is a function of a leader's coaching
and a motivated constituent**

I have never met an effective leader that was not an effective coach. My next theory is not all-inclusive. In other words, you may discover, or have discovered, functions that need to be added. But if this makes you think about your intentional efforts to become a better leader through being a better coach, it has served its purpose. Angela Duckworth, in her book *Grit: The Power of Passion and Perseverance,* introduces a theory that got me thinking. Consider her theory:

Skill: f(talent + effort)
Accomplishment: f(skill + effort)

When considering skill and accomplishment, the common variable is *effort*. It seems reasonable that effort needs to be measured by how it is directed and its intensity. The intensity of the effort is measured by how motivated one is. How the effort is directed, at least in part, is measured by the effectiveness of coaching received. Hence, effective leadership means, in part, effective coaching.

I watched a basketball game on TV and heard the commentator say about one of the players, "Boy, that kid has talent." Talent is God-given. Whatever talents you have, you are born with. Though the basketball player is talented, to be sure, the announcer implied that the player exerted much effort to develop his talents. Without such effort, the player would fall far below his potential. With some effort, he transforms his talent into skill. With more effort he transforms his skill into extraordinary accomplishment.

Effort is the common variable embedded in skill and accomplishment. Though Duckworth addresses the inner drive of an individual, I am extending this theory to engage a leader's impact on the variable of *effort*. The relevance of this theory rests, at least in part, in the leader's success in motivating and coaching their followers. Motivation puts a desire to extend an "effort" into the hearts of the follower. Coaching (which can extend learning) imparts knowledge that engages the brain in such a way that it makes the "effort" optimally applied. Together, coaching and motivating engage the heart with the mind. This section talks about coaching as an important extension to transformational leadership, the subject of Section 3. Section 5 explores how leaders can motivate followers. This section will bring you on a reflective journey to make you an effective coach and maybe even a mentor.

28. The Case for Coaching

Katy was a new girl at her school in Savannah, Georgia. She had just moved into the area, was 13 years old, and in the 7th grade. She was little, not much of an athlete, and an average student. Often teased and demeaned by her classmates, she tried to make friends but unfortunately had few. She tried out for the basketball team and got cut, ran the quarter mile at athletic day and came in 11th out of 12, and tried to invite other girls to her house to play. When they did not come, her feeling of depression began to set in.

Coach Kirkley was Katy's physical education teacher in addition to his duties as the boys' head basketball coach. He saw the pain and potential in this little girl. Coach Kirkley's only formal contact with Katy came through his physical education class, but in Katy's mind he was her coach. It was Coach who inspired her to stay focused and believe in herself. Maybe it was his kind and encouraging words, informal recognition in front of others, or getting to know Katy's family in such a way so he could better support this little girl, but support and encourage her he did.

Several years later, Katy and her family moved to a city six hours away. At age 16, Katy's mother unexpectedly died, and it was Coach Kirkley who drove the six hours to spend several days continuing to be the coach who cared. It was Coach Kirkley who went to a cross country meet four hours north of Savannah to watch Katy run when she was a senior in high school. There were 422 contestants that day—Katy finished 22nd. Katy would later attend Texas Christian University, a Division I school, make the cross-country team, and run in a Conference USA championship.

To date she has run in seven marathons, including the Boston Marathon. She would graduate with a master's degree in international business from Sussex University in London, marry and have two wonderful children. Today, she owns a very successful financial business, is president of her local Kiwanis Club, is on the Board of Directors of several nonprofit institutions, is a leader in her church, and yes, she still runs. One cannot measure the impact Coach Kirkley had, and still has, on her life.

I wonder how many other "Katys" are out there who have been directly impacted by this coach? One example is a fiery and emotional assistant coach whose language and aggressive behavior would have certainly gotten him fired and possibly ended his career if it were not for Coach Kirkley and his mentoring. Today that assistant is married, is a father, and is realizing a successful coaching career in Atlanta. He is calmer and seems to focus on the heart of the individual. He realizes that everyone has value and is important, independent of their athletic skills. Sounds like Coach Kirkley.

Another example is a young woman who graduated from Coach Kirkley's school. After several years in college, it became apparent she was suffering from bulimia. Again, it was Coach who made the trip, knocked on the door, and continued to do what he does. Today that woman not only survived, but is a wife, a mother, and is a successful high school cross country head coach in South Carolina, having coached teams to three state championships.

Stories like these represent thousands of individuals impacted by this coach and all the other great coaches in our communities. This greatness comes from a selfless effort to make others better. These great coaches understand that it is not enough to inspire those being coached to believe in their leadership, or even the team. They inspire those they coach to also believe in themselves. Their reward is knowing they made a difference in the life of an individual. It puts humility in its greatest context.

I can assure you that any motive Coach Kirkley has had did not include any recognition for himself, instead he celebrates the recognition of others to raise them up so they could understand their great potential. All these people Coach impacted had talent. It was effort to develop that talent that gave them skill and further effort to improve on skill, evolving into wonderful accomplishment. Coaching was integral to inspiring and channeling effort.

Effective coaching, as a leader (or teacher for that matter), means that you truly care about the person you are coaching or mentoring. Your priority lies with their learning, often times subordinating a more self-serving agenda like winning or accomplishing corporate/institutional goals. Over the years, we all have had teachers, bosses, coworkers, and even members of our family who cared about us and some who did not.

Think about the boss you respected versus the one you did not. The selfless boss, the one you respected, I suspect placed your learning as important. She was probably a very effective coach. I would guess that one of his values was "respect for the individual." As opposed to the self-serving boss, the one you did not respect, probably did not care about your learning, hence his coaching had little (if any) effect. The learning that did take place was on your own or from respected peers.

As we discussed in Section 3 (Transformational Leadership), if we are in environments that are constantly changing, then we must be constantly learning. Leaders must take responsibility for establishing a learning culture and that means being effective coaches. That effectiveness starts with selflessly caring for and respecting those we lead.

Great coaches seem to have several things in common. First, we trust them. That trust starts with us believing that they truly care about our development and well-being and thus are prepared, inwardly, to coach selflessly. Second, they show they are competent. They "know their stuff." They are competent as leaders and competent in their subject matter. They are learners as well as teachers. Third, they have a process to their coaching. In other words, their coaching is organized and intentional. Fourth, they possess character, implying they have the courage to pass judgment as to the merits, or not, of our professional performance. They are not shy about having those difficult conversations. This judgment is meant to make us better, not motivated by judgmentalism.

29. Getting Yourself Ready to Coach

Effective Coaches Are Credible

Credibility: f(trust and competency)

Being credible boils down to affirmatively answering the following two questions:
1. Can I be trusted?
2. Am I justifiably perceived as being competent in the field for which I am coaching?'

Can I Be Trusted?

Well, can you? If you answer, "yes," then what is it about you that you should be trusted? Trust centers around being able to authentically express and model the tenets of what you believe in. Hence it is impossible to discuss what you believe in without being able to express your values and purpose clearly and authentically. Core to effective coaching is having an overarching purpose that includes the success of the one being coached and having a set of values that serve as instruments as to how you behave and make decisions. These are the subjects of the first two sections of this book, and I would suggest that if you are not clear, to yourself, as to what your purpose is and what your values are, go back and reread those sections. The self-reflection inspired by these first sections will help you discover your purpose and values. Being trusted as a coach stem from purpose, values, and authentic articulation and modeling.

Lieutenant Colonel (LTC) Ted Gibblet was a 20-year Army veteran assigned as a Professor of Military Science at the University of Wisconsin. He had been in the assignment for over a year when I arrived as a captain, more than ten years junior to LTC Gibblet. LTC Gibblet was responsible for teaching leadership, as I was, and for recruiting students into the university's ROTC program. He was my boss. ROTC recruiting was failing miserably, and within days of my arrival he delegated all recruiting responsibility to me. Within several months he was becoming very critical of my progress and made it clear that I was responsible for the success *or failure* of the program's recruiting results.

I began teaching leadership to freshmen and sophomore level students. I sprinkled military stories into the leadership lessons. We talked about the leadership lessons learned in the recent Grenada invasion, my leadership experiences as a young lieutenant in Alaska, commanding a company of soldiers in the Presidential Honor Guard in Washington D.C. (known in military circles as the "Old Guard"), and stories about negotiating Ranger School and becoming a US Army Ranger.

Many students got engaged with learning leadership through these military stories. From these classes a significant number of students joined the ROTC program. Within a year, the recruiting program had completely turned around and was ranked at the top of the region.

LTC Gibblet made efforts to take sole credit for this accomplishment though he had very little to do with the success. He wanted to take credit (and tried) rather than give credit. He wanted respect from others without giving respect to others. I had no idea what he really believed in. I can only guess that his values revolved around himself, with little regard for me or anyone else for that matter. I did not trust him.

Am I Competent?

Competency centers on learning. Establishing a learning culture, as discussed in Section 3, means that everyone, including the leader, take personal responsibility for individual learning. Being able to negotiate change means learning is an "all the time" effort. With learning comes competency, the second variable to being credible and becoming an effective coach.

LTC Gibblet failed at developing and leading an effective recruiting program. Worse yet, he did not learn from this failure. Instead, he tried to take credit for a now successful program — credit he did not deserve. He was not competent.

It is important to point out, however, he *could have been* a successful coach. LTC Gibblet approached success as if it were a commodity rather than a coordinated effort of talent, effort, and skill. He approached failure as a sign of incompetence that needed to be covered up, rather than it being an opportunity to learn. He could have partnered with me, and together we could have learned more and achieved even better results. Maybe I could have learned something from his experience, and he could have learned from me, despite me being junior to him and him being my boss.

He could have recognized my accomplishment and the accomplishments of others, thus inspiring an even greater effort from the team. We could have gotten to know each other better—learn each other's values, what was important to us as individuals, and appreciated each other's purpose. Together, we may have been better, but we will never know. His self-serving nature and insecurities prevented him from being ready to coach.

Getting ready to coach can be difficult. You have to be ready to give and to care without expecting anything in return except effort. LTC Gibblet was concerned primarily with how he was perceived. His focus was on what he could get. Coach Kirkley prepared himself as a selfless provider of modeling and knowledge. His focus was on what he could give.

30. Self-Awareness

Along with values and purpose, understanding our own motivations, strengths, and weaknesses are key to preparing for coaching and mentoring. This knowledge of self inspires a humble self-confidence that was missing in LTC Gibblet and other leaders exampled in this book who were not effective. The self-confidence associated with recognizing one's limitations and faults, but not at the expense of recognizing one's positive qualities, contributes to a self-confident humility usually associated with great coaches, mentors, and leaders.

Coach Kirkley, Rob (the boss who gave me credit for his idea), and Mrs. Carney (fifth grade teacher) had this combination of humility and self-confidence. LTC Gibblet, Frank (the self-serving financial boss), and Mrs. Schultz (4th grade teacher) did not. Deep reflections on self, what really motivates you (the subject of Section 5) and discovering your purpose and values (Sections 1 and 2) will inspire a greater understanding of your strengths and weaknesses and are essential to self-awareness and preparing to be a coach or mentor.

Motives are at the center of successful coaching and mentoring. Rob, Mrs. Carney, and Coach Kirkley had one thing in common—they never went into their positions with a motive of seeing what they could *get*. Rather their primary motive was on what they could *give*. Any self-serving agenda was second behind doing what was best for those they were leading and coaching. They put the needs of others ahead of their own. Their focus was on raising others up, even at their own personal expense.

A person consumed with self will not consider raising those they are coaching up as their top priority and will not be as effective. Self-awareness (discovering your strengths and weaknesses, motivations, and values) is important to having the humble self-confidence associated with making others the priority.

Getting ready to coach is no different than getting ready to lead. Consider the following:

1. People want to be coached and mentored by people who believe in something they can relate to. What coaches represent is something that their followers can believe in and learn from. That means great coaches, like great leaders, have reflected on and internalized a purpose that drives their direction and a set of values that guide decisions and behaviors. They can be trusted.

2. Great coaches are great learners. They are comfortable in their own skin and learn from their mistakes and even advertise those mistakes so that those being coached can also learn. They partner with the ones being coached to form a team whose only focus is to improve the ones being coached. Through this learning they take their competency seriously.

3. Great coaches are authentic. They authentically express and model their values. This transparency transcends into serving as examples as to how to behave, make

decisions, and conduct their professional lives. This authentism represents to those being coached why they deserve to be coached by these leaders.

31. Coaching Versus Mentoring

Consider David and Rob

Coaching and mentoring are kindred spirits. Though the terms are often used interchangeably, they are not the same. Leaders are responsible for the development of their constituents in such ways that improve performance. That development usually includes helping fill the skill and knowledge gaps associated with a certain position or responsibility. Mentors focus on future growth beyond the immediate circumstances. Mentors need coaching skills to help identify the skill and knowledge gaps.

A mentored relationship extends this coaching relationship to address learning goals that will move the person into their future in a productive and effective way. Coaching is more specific and usually associated with progression towards a specific task or skill. This is essential for effective leadership. Mentoring is a deeper relationship that requires full appreciation and acceptance from both parties. Mentoring is a sacred task, and a mentoring relationship is not easy to develop. Let me give an example.

Have you ever led someone you did not like? For whatever reason—attitude, different values, personal respect not rendered to a comfortable level, or maybe it was something you just couldn't put a finger on. Some people are just difficult to like. Not liking a constituent does not mean you cannot lead them. Consider David.

David was a successful financial advisor that I was responsible for leading, but he tended to be insubordinate to the point of demeaning me and others on the leadership team. At one point his behavior was hurting morale and challenging my authority as his supervisor. One Friday afternoon, after he failed to attend one of my few mandatory meetings, I told him that his insubordinate behavior would not be tolerated. Using profanity, he told me that he did not have to do anything that I asked of him. This was not the first time he portrayed this attitude in front of others.

I demanded his key to the office and fired him. If he refused to be coached, he could not be influenced, and I could not lead him. One of us had to go, and it was going to be him. I ordered him to leave the premise. Though he was fired, I asked my operations manager to inform David that if he wanted to be interviewed by me with the possibility of being reinstated, I would see him in my office at 10 a.m. the following Monday. I would give him one hour to convince me that I could coach/lead him. This gave David the weekend to think about what he wanted to do and to reflect on what he had done.

That Monday he came in, apologized, and we set up a productive coaching process where we would talk on a scheduled basis about ways that he could improve. I reinstated him on a probationary basis. Our relationship improved. He took my suggestions, and his skill and knowledge gaps began to fill. As I look back, I have concluded that our values were quite different when it came to respecting others. I did not like the way he treated other coworkers. I really did not like David. Despite this, I concluded I could still coach him because he allowed it and I was willing. Our values were somewhat aligned in that he was a person of integrity and he put the best interests of his clients first. I would never be his mentor, but if he was to continue in this organization, he had to allow me to influence him and that meant coach him. Sometimes leadership is messy. Now, consider Rob.

Rob was responsible for running a division for Merrill Lynch located in the central part of the country. He had invited me on several occasions to be a guest speaker in his offices. Generally, I would speak on strategies to developing a successful financial advisory business. I later left that role to become a manager with the responsibility of leading a region comprised of financial advisors and a supporting infrastructure. Some years after assuming a management role exclusively, Rob actually became my boss, and I was responsible for running one of the several regions under his control.

By the nature of his position, he was my coach. Now years later, long after we left those positions, we continue to exchange ideas and talk. Overtime, he became my mentor. Becoming my mentor went beyond a mutual respect we had for one another. Our values were closely aligned. He authored a coaching process where we communicated on an organized and intentional basis. A mentoring relationship evolved out of that process. This process focused on coaching and intended to help in my development as well as the development of all those who reported directly to him. He called this process *supernova*. I adopted supernova in my organization. Because of supernova, I became a more effective coach that, in some cases, evolved into a mentoring relationship.

32. Supernova

A Coaching Process

Supernovas are rare and spectacular. They occur when a massive star, often eight times larger than the sun, has exhausted its nuclear fuel that holds the mass together. The mass is no longer sustainable. The star explodes and contracts to a much smaller size that is brighter and hotter than the original star. The analogy is beautiful to coaching and mentoring. The supernova concept portrays an intentional segmentation, organization, and plan for coaching and possibly mentoring. It focuses energy on the development of others, allowing those we are responsible for to "explode" with the realization of their great potential.

Too many times coaching is a haphazard affair associated with annual reviews and nonscheduled and informal conversations about the challenges of the day. The supernova process emphasizes the importance of structure in coaching in the workplace. This structure is critical to having a learning culture—the subject of Section 3. The learner is the person being coached and developed.

Early in this process, the learner's primary focus may not be on development. Rather it may be socialization or an attitude of just going along with what the boss wants. Initially, that is not important. What *is* important is the intent of the coach, or mentor, to put the development of those being coached, or mentored, on center stage. The intentional process is pivotal to realizing development for the learner. The supernova process frames who will be coached, or mentored (segmentation), how communication will be conducted (organization), and what is hoped to be achieved by this effort (the plan).

Segmentation

If change is constant, and learning is the principal strategy to negotiate a constantly changing environment, then it stands to reason that the most critical function of the leader is to create environments where learning is constant. A natural corollary to learning is coaching. Every leader is responsible for coaching every person who directly reports to them. Thus, selecting whom you coach (segmentation) is simply those who report directly to you. Expect from leaders who report to you a coaching relationship between them and those who report to them. The span of who reports to whom takes on new meaning when you schedule monthly coaching sessions, for example. To assess capacity, or how many you can coach, should influence how many one can be responsible to lead. Your success as a coach to those who report to you will be largely realized by your credibility (trust and competence). Effective coaching enhances mutual credibility.

In David's case (remember—the insubordinate financial advisor I fired then rehired), his potential to be coached was a critical criterion for him being retained. To lead someone, you must be in a position to influence them. As I have repeated, effective coaching is a principal activity for influencing and thus leading. If David reported to me, I had to be in a position to coach. To be effective as

David's coach meant I had to be reasonably credible (trustworthy and competent). However, this also works in reverse. To be effective as David's coach meant he had to be reasonably credible to me. If someone reports to you where credibility is missing, either him being credible to you, or you being credible to him, your ability to coach and influence is significantly reduced. If you make the decision not to coach someone who reports to you, that means someone must go, you or him.

In David's case it was going to be him (the boss is usually, but not always, retained). Fortunately, we were able to establish a degree of credibility between us for me to effectively coach and influence, and thus lead, him.

Organization

Supernova organization is simple and direct. It focuses on two critical aspects of coaching and mentoring. First is a scheduled meeting, I suggest minimally monthly, at the same time for each meeting. For example, coaching/mentoring sessions will begin at 10:00 a.m. the second Tuesday of each month and will last one hour. The supervisor and the direct report can put this on their calendars for the entire year. The second is a structured record keeping system that each partner keeps that includes personal information, goals, expectations, and accountability.

The scheduled meetings may seem obvious, but its brilliance is in its simplicity. Let me explain by giving two examples. First, Frank was my boss for several years. Remember he was the boss in Section 2 who tried to take credit for other's accomplishments and work. We would talk periodically. If I needed to talk to him, usually after several attempts, we would finally connect. Maybe some coaching would emerge, but it was accidental and unintended, from my perspective. The few times we met in person (maybe once or twice a year) it was not uncommon to be interrupted numerous times.

When Rob replaced Frank, scheduled meetings were put in place. These were monthly meetings that lasted one hour and took place at the same time each month. Once a quarter the meeting would be in person or be skyped. There were no interruptions. It was our time to be together. During our early time of putting this in place, I remember calling Rob about a matter I needed his opinion on. We exchanged messages, and finally we connected. He gave his view and then reminded me that our scheduled meeting was next week. Rather than chasing each other down, why not wait for our meeting if the issues could wait? Think of the time saved and increased efficiency. It was so simple but so brilliant.

The second component to the organization was the record keeping. Both Frank and Rob kept records of our meetings. Frank's records were kept in a manila file that was organized according to organizational goals. Examples of organizational goals would be new business, hiring, financial plans completed, profit margins, etc. Rob's records were more complex. Certainly, organizational expectations were a part of the file but also included were items that were helpful for positively impacting my individual development.

Rob's file had two parts. The left side was the static side (things that seldom changed) that included the following:

1. Name, address, phone number
2. Names of wife/husband and children (with children's ages and maybe some notes on special interests such as important extracurricular activities of children/wife or husband).
3. Personal and professional goals.

4. The five most important things in their lives.
5. Purposes and values if they have been discovered or as they become discovered

The right side of the file contained ongoing recorded notes with more dynamic and adjustable information. This part may include the following:

1. Progress on short-term goals established in recent coaching sessions.
2. Certain things for which I am being held accountable.
3. A review on how I am progressing on personal goals.
4. Problems or concerns that need to be raised.
5. Solution or progress on problems previously raised. These are normally professional problems but can also include personal problems if appropriate.

I would suggest you consider the seven important aspects to developing those for whom you are responsible according to John Maxwell's book (2008), *Mentoring 101: What Every Leader Needs to Know*:

1. Development is a long-term process. As we discussed earlier, we are in an environment that is constantly changing, which means we are constantly learning. Learning and changing take time, but to recognize the need to learn and change is important to accepting a process of development. This acceptance should include notes in the file that specifically state that supervisor and follower have entered an intentional coaching relationship.
2. Discover each person's dreams and goals. In coaching and leadership, we teach people what they need to know

to do a job. This may be important in achieving organizational goals such as promotions, pay raises, and so forth. However, development is based on needs. Maxwell states: "You give them what they need in order to become better people. To do that well, you need to know their dreams and desires." Recording goals and ensuring a system of score keeping is an important part of *coaching* organization. Sharing and recording real personal dreams is an important part of *mentoring*.

3. Be fair but not equal. In other words, lead everyone differently. The structure of the organization may be the same for everyone, but the content is different. Rookie leaders make this mistake. They try to lead everyone the same. People learn differently and have different needs. It is fair but not necessarily equal.

4. Use organizational goals for individual development. We discussed this earlier. Rob did this; Frank did not. Keep score. For example, in coaching a follower to develop appropriate tactics and strategies to accomplish organizational goals, we must always be reminded that learning is central to coaching. When someone learns, they are *developed as individuals*. Learning cannot be taken away, but it can be expanded with good coaching and maturity.

5. Help them know themselves. Record, verbatim, what is said that you feel is significant. It will come in handy in later discussions when you quote them. As I have said, often the one being coached or mentored does not know himself as well as he may think. In addition, I assume that they are even better than they think. It is part of helping them better understand their potential. That

assumption is helpful in them discovering how much potential they really have.

6. Be ready to have hard conversations. Learning is not easy. Challenges and even some failure can occur. These are positive opportunities for learning and growth. Record detailed notes of these discussions, for that will be important for celebrating successes later. Effectively conducting hard conversations is so important I have reserved a separate chapter.

7. Celebrate the right wins. Accomplishing the organizational goals is important when coaching someone who reports to you. These are tactical victories. However, when mentoring, it is the strategic victories that have value. It is these victories that give incentives for people to learn, grow, and eventually realize their great potential. This highlights the accountability to goals and their importance in record keeping.

Value discovery is integral in the coaching and mentoring process. Remember that a portion of the left side of the record keeping folder is dedicated to recording personal values as they are shared or discovered. In the first few meetings, everyone would be well served to share with each other and record the five most important things in each other's lives. Usually you will find family, spirituality, health, job, and so forth, on these lists. However, it is important not to assume. Remember, the operations manager in Florida, Marge? Her number two was her cat! Who would have known? Also included on the left side (static side) of the folder are notes on values. Sharing discovered values is critical to forming a base for your relationship. Consider the four critical questions posed in Section 2 to explore individual values:

1. What core values (values that you would hold regardless of whether they were rewarded) do you personally bring to work?
2. How have your core values changed over the course of your life?
3. What values would you tell your children or the most significant people in your life that you hold at work and that you hope they would also hold?
4. If you had one hour to live, and you have the people you love the most in front of you. These are your last and most important words you will ever say to them and will form your legacy. What would you say?

It is also important to investigate values alignment with the organization and the coaching/mentoring partnership. Questions that could be helpful are:

1. If you were to start a new organization in a different line of work, what core values would you build into your new organization, regardless of industry?
2. What are the current values of this organization?
3. What core values does your organization need to adapt to lead to a bright future?

Even a greater context for these questions can be found in Johnson's 2007 book *Ethics in the Workplace.*

As a supervisor, if your discussions answer these questions in an intimate way, and both partners share honestly their answers, and there is evidence of values alignment, I would argue that a wonderful opportunity for productive mentoring exists. At a minimum, a greater degree of transparency will evolve, giving opportunity for more effective coaching.

We have organized a coaching and mentoring framework that is composed of dedicated time and a record keeping system that logs intimate conversations and decisions with the supervisory relationship. We have discussed supervisory coaching as a critical element to effective leadership that all direct reports deserve from their supervisors. We have also discovered the need to keep a watchful eye for mentoring opportunities that focus more on realizing one's human potential. Now we need a coaching plan.

Planning

"Planning is based on values, not just increasing value."
— **Rob Knapp in his book** *Supernova*

Nancy was struggling as the COO of a large nonprofit agency in the Chattanooga area. The CEO asked me to coach her. I set up a time, and we met. I was reasonably organized, had my file set up, and looked forward to helping her in her position. The problem was that although we had a series of "nice discussions," we never really formatted our discussions as previously described and, before long, I received notice that she resigned her position. In all honesty, it was probably a helpless cause in that I sensed that Nancy's impression of me was that my efforts were not to help her but to help the CEO build a case for dismissing her. Maybe if we had set up a plan based on realizing purpose and being governed by a set of values, she would have trusted me more and the outcome would have been different. Instead of nice conversations, maybe we could have focused our discussions on Nancy's development.

Organizations are famous for custom covers, beautifully organized folders, and "nice conversations." I have done it myself.

Knapp, in his book *Supernova*, defines planning as "meaning with deadlines." The conversations that the organization generates converts to implementation of action and activities that planning generates. Well-organized coaching evolves into plans of action where behavior is changed. The changing of behavior is motivated by deadlines. This is what was missing with my relationship with Nancy.

From this organized coaching effort, a focus can evolve. This coaching, maybe disguised as conversations, can be rich and meaningful with a focus. When generated, you are establishing an intimacy that makes your coaching or mentoring very effective. Out of the organization can emerge a plan for learning, growth, and accomplishment that is intentional. The key is to apply deadlines to behavioral changes as measured by an agreed upon "ruler." The plan then emerges. Remember, the purpose of coaching is not to conduct therapy, rather it is to inspire behavioral changes that fills the "gaps" that improve performance.

Finally, it is important to understand that we must allow plans to form. Patience is important. When I was coaching Nancy, I was focused on behavioral changes too soon. Some have referred this to a "microwave" mindset. This is the expectation of reaping instant results. I am not implying that deadlines for behavioral changes should not be encouraged quickly. I am implying that we should expect some challenges along the way. We are not looking for opportunities to be critical with those being coached, rather we are looking for learning.

This brings us back to values alignment and why it is so important. When entering a coaching relationship, values alignment is key to mutual trust (hence credibility).

In mentoring you must ask: Are you willing to persevere with someone on this type of journey? Organization is important, but without the evolution of the plan, the process becomes the program. It is the journey with the person that evolves into real results that can be life changing.

Remember, in the introduction I introduced you to the manager of the fitness facility I owned. Remember he had problems working with women which concerned me. After some coaching attempts, I felt compelled to terminate his employment for cause. It was a difficult conversation. At his request I continued to be his mentor. The reason was because, except for my value of "Respect for the Individual," our values were reasonably aligned. We both had similar definitions for being "Christ Centered," having "integrity," and displaying "responsible citizenship." We both felt I could make a difference in his life over the long term if I stayed involved.

We had a plan that unfolded, and we both decided that we wanted to see the plan through until the end. It has been a long journey for him with several job changes and a divorce. Mentoring continued through these transitions. Behavioral changes finally emerged, and he appears to be on a road of success. It has been five years. What kept me involved was our aligned values. However, the real work started after the difficult conversation when I fired him.

33. A Difficult Conversation

The Battle of Gettysburg was one of the deadliest events in American history. Casualties exceeded fifty thousand. The movie *Gettysburg* depicts the events of this battle. In the movie, Martin Sheen plays General Robert E. Lee, Commander of the Confederate Army, and Joseph Fuqua plays Major General Jeb Stuart, Commander of the Confederate Cavalry. History, and the movie, indicate trouble between Stuart and Lee. The Cavalry, commanded by Stuart, had a primary mission of being the "eyes and ears" of the Confederate army. The Cavalry's principal mission was to report the enemy's troop movements, position, and other intelligence information so commanders, like Lee, could make informed decisions.

Unfortunately, General Stuart had been publicly embarrassed, and his ego hurt, when the Southern press advertised him being taken by surprise in battle at Brandy Station. He began a campaign of his own to restore his public reputation well south of Gettysburg, abandoning his primary mission of providing critical intelligence. This forced Lee to make decisions without critical information. Hence Stuart failed in his mission of reporting needed intelligence. The movie depicts the difficult conversation between Lee and Stuart that can serve as a model as to how we could conduct difficult conversation. Before we dissect the conversation, I would suggest you Google "movie Gettysburg Lee and Stuart" and spend a few minutes to review this scene.

With the help of Peter Bregman's book (2018), *Leading with Emotional Courage*, I have developed a checklist for conducting a difficult conversation. I would suggest reviewing this checklist prior to such conversations:

1. What outcome do you want to achieve?
   a. Negate haphazard outcomes.
   b. Connect the outcome to the realization of the overarching purpose and/or organization's values.
   c. As Lee did with Stuart, state a clear understanding of the shortcoming.
   d. State the consequences of this shortcoming.
   e. Make this a learning opportunity.

2. Deal with the facts when communicating outcomes that are not debatable.
   a. For example, "I am hurt that you…" rather than "I can't believe that you…" Me being hurt is a fact.
   b. "I have been informed by people I respect that you…" Again, you being informed is a fact.
   c. In Lee's case, he states, "It is the opinion of some highly respected officers that you…"
   d. Lee stated, "You failed in your mission." This is a fact in that Stuart needed to keep Lee informed, and he did not.

3. How should you communicate to achieve the desired outcome?
   a. First, lead with the punchline. Understand they do not

know the hardship and toll you have gone through to have this conversation, and this gives context to the conversation.

b. Without this lead, you are in danger of having an extended conversation without an understanding as to why the conversation is even taking place. Some examples of leading punchlines are, "Thanks for coming in. Bill, I have decided not to select you as the manager for Team A and I want you to know why." "Thanks for coming in Sue. I am getting feedback from people I respect that you are disrupting the workplace by yelling at team members, coming in late, or not doing your fair share. Let me give you some specific examples…

c. Give a purpose for the conversation. As an example, "My purpose for talking to you is to figure a plan of corrective behaviors."

4. How do you remind them of their skill to do the job?
   a. If appropriate, after the punchline and the initial emotional response that can take place, remind the person of their skills, why they were hired, and their exceptional potential that still resides in them.
   b. Remind them that you expect them to take this information and learn from it, "like any quality professional" (or something more appropriate given the position of the person). In Lee's case he states, "I expect you to learn from this like a man does."

5. Be clear about consequences.
   a. Lee states, "This can never, never happen again." For those that have been in the military or in the corporate

sector, this more than implies that the follower will be replaced if this happens again.

b. In communicating the consequences, it is important to remind them that you are holding them accountable for certain actions and behaviors, and there are consequences.

Difficult conversabtions are integral to a leader being an effective coach. Part of this conversation, or maybe another conversation, you enter into a process of accountability. In holding someone accountable I have found it sometimes helpful to review the following accountability checklist:

1. Clear expectations.
    a. Be clear about the expected outcome and how that outcome relates to the organization's purpose. Maybe how the outcome relates to 'the big arrow' in Section 1.
    b. This clarity should include how you measure success.
    c. This needs to be a two-way conversation so everyone is on the same page.
    d. Ask the person to summarize the main points. I would encourage this to be written down.

2. Clear Capability.
    a. What skills does the person need to be successful? Does the person have those skills?
    b. If not, develop a developmental plan for this person to gain those skills or allow access to a teammate who has the skills to assist.

    c. What resources are needed for success? Are those resources available, or do they need to be acquired?

3. Clear measurement.
   a. Being clear on how success will be measured prevents being surprised by failure.
   b. When results or work begin to fall short, an early warning can inspire help.
   c. A culture that intimidates or makes asking for help a sign of weakness is a leadership concern and needs to be remedied. The remedy usually includes a consistent and open dialogue.
   d. During the "expectation conversation," agree on weekly conversations that address milestones that are clear and measurable; assess delivering on commitments; assess working well with others; assess capability (coaching, needed team participation, and weekly feedback).
   e. Remember, it is more important to be helpful than nice.

4. Clear feedback.
   a. This must be honest, open, and ongoing.
   b. Make sure they know clearly where they stand.
   c. Feedback should be fact based and easy to deliver.
   d. Feedback must be a two-way street. What can you do to be more helpful? Feedback sessions demand preparation by both parties.

5. Clear consequences.
   a. If you have been clear in your expectations, coaching, and genuine willingness to support these efforts you can

be confident that you did your part to support acceptable performance.

b. After expectations can be evaluated for success, you have three choices: repeat, reward, release.

   i. Repeat the steps if you feel there was a lack of clarity.

   ii. If there is success, reward appropriately through acknowledgement, promotion, etc.

   iii. If the person has not proven to be accountable and you have followed these steps, then they are not a good fit. Change roles or release.

34. Concluding Thoughts and Action Steps on Coaching

I have never met an effective leader that was not a good coach. Mentoring is an evolution of the coaching effort, but it is not essential to effective leadership. Coaching *is* essential. This section challenges you on three levels. First, you get yourself ready to coach by having discovered your personal purpose and values and by always making an effort to learn, thereby showing competency. This is critical to credibility and maybe establishing some common ground with the one being coached. Second, you have a coaching process that is intentional. I recommend the Supernova process. Third; do not shy away from difficult conversations. Make sure you are organized by reviewing the difficult conversation and accountability checklist.

Get yourself ready to coach.

1. Good coaches are credible, implying they can be trusted and are competent.
   a. To be trusted means that you have a set of values and a personal purpose that drives your decisions and behaviors. If you have difficulty stating your purpose and

values, it is important you revisit Sections 1 and 2 of this book. These sections form the basis for your credibility. As a quick review, discovering your personal purpose, Section 1:

- Start with listing the five most important things in your life. Knowing what is important to you and sharing this with the one you are coaching will allow them to feel free to do the same, and a bond can form.
- Place what is important to you in categories. For example, wife, children, grandchildren, relationship with Christ, to be healthy, to be the best nurse, or professor, or leader, or…
- Define your role in impacting what is important.
- Ask yourself three separate times "Why is this important?" As you ask this question, your purpose will begin to be discovered.
- Review Section 1 again if you have not had some evidence as to your life's purpose.

b. Review discovering your values by answering these questions presented in Section 2:

- What core values (values that you would hold regardless of whether they were rewarded) do you personally bring to your work?
- What core values would you tell your children that you hold at work and that you hope they will hold as working adults?
- If you were to start a new organization in a different line of work, what core values would you build into the new organization, regardless of the industry.

- If you had one hour to live and you had the most important people in your life in front of you, what would you say? What you say they will never forget. It is what will guide them during their tough times. It will be your legacy and be repeated to people they deeply love.
- Review Section 2 again if you have not had some evidence as to discovering your personal values

c. List your great strengths and your weaknesses as you perceive them. Remember the self-confidence associated with recognizing one's limitations and faults, but not at the expense of recognizing one's positive qualities contributes to a self-confident humility usually associated with great coaches and mentors (and leaders).

Develop Your Coaching Process

1. Segmentation
   a. Whom are you coaching?
   b. Ensure leaders that report to you are clear about whom they are coaching and their coaching responsibilities.

2. Organization
   a. Schedule intentional coaching sessions.
   b. Structure your record keeping.
   c. Review the contents of the records being guided by the suggestions in Chapter 32. Be sure to include what is important.

3. Planning

a. Planning is meaning with deadlines.
b. Conversations convert to actions and activities that planning generates.
c. Planning emerges from meaningful conversations but planning also takes patience. Plans must be allowed to form.

A Difficult Conversation

1. Before the conversation, review your checklist presented in Chapter 33:
   a. What outcome do you want to achieve?
   b. What do you communicate to achieve the outcome?
   c. How should you communicate to achieve the desired outcome?
   d. Remind the person of their skill, why they were hired, and their potential.

2. Often accountability should be imbedded in these conversations. Review the accountability checklist in Chapter 36:
   a. Clear expectations
   b. Clear capability
   c. Clear measurement
   d. Clear feedback
   e. Clear consequences

Contributing Work
to Section 4

This work helped inspire some
of the key concepts

Bell, C. (2000). "The Mentor as a Partner," *Training and Development, 54*(2), 7.

Buford, B. *Halftime: Changing Your Game Plan from Successful to Significant* (Grand Rapids, MI: Zondervan), 1994.

Collins, J. C. *Good to Great: Why Some Companies Make the Leap-- and Others Don't* (New York: Harper Business), 2001.

Cooper, T. D. *Making Judgements without Being Judgmental* (Madison, WI: InterVarsity Press), 2006.

D'Abate, C., Eddy, E., & Tannenbaum, S. (2003). "What's in a Name? A Literature-based Approach to Understanding Mentoring, Coaching, and Other Constructs That Describe Developmental Interactions." *Human Resource Development Review, 2*(4), 24. doi: 10.117/1534484303255033

Drucker, P. "Managing Oneself." *Harvard Business Review*, 13, 1999.

Fullan, M., *The Six Secrets of Change* (San Fransisco, CA: Josse-Bass), 2008.

Hughes, R., Ginnett, R., & Curphy, G. *Leadership: Enhancing the Lessons of Experience* (7th ed.) (New York: McGraw Hill Companies, Inc.), 2012.

Johnson, C. *Meeting the Ethical Challenge of Leadership: Casting Light or Shadow* (4 ed.) (Thousand Oaks, CA: Sage Publications, Inc.), 2012.

Knapp, R. *The Supernova Advisor* (Hoboken, NJ: John Wiley & Sons, Inc.), 2008.

Bergman, P. *Leading with Emotional Courage* (Hoboken, NJ, John Wiley and Sons, Inc.), 2018.

Martin. *The Opposable Mind: How Successful Leaders Win through Integrative Thinking* (Boston, MA: Harvard Business School), 2007.

Maxwell, J. *Mentoring 101: What Every Leader Needs to Know* (Nashville, TN: Thomas Nelson, Inc.), 2008.

Miloff, M., & Zachary, L. "Mentoring to Develop Strategic Leaders." *T + D*, 66(4), 3, 2012.

Shea, G. "Can a Supervisor Mentor?" *Supervision,* 56 (November), 4, 1985.

Stoddard, D., & Tamasy, R. *The Heart of Mentoring: Ten Proven Principles for Developing People to their Fullest Potential.* (Colorado Springs, CO: NavPress), 2003.

Zachary, L. *A Mentors Guide: Facilitating Effective Learning Relationships* (2 ed.) (San Francisco, CA: Jossey-Bass), 2012.

Senge, P. (2006), *The Fifth Dimension: The Art and Practice of Learning Organizations* (New York: Doubleday), 2006.

19. Stevenson, L., & Haberman, D., *The Ten Theories of Human Nature* (5 ed.). (New York: Oxford University Press), 2009.

Section 5

Motivation — Inspiring the Heart
You Are a Motivator Already

Effective Effort: f (A leader's coaching
+ A motivated constituent)

Effort is a function of a leader's coaching and a motivated constituent

The theories postulated in the first four sections of this book can be important in inspiring the hearts of your constituents. If you are applying these theories, then you are a motivator already. A unifying purpose, aligned values, transformational dynamics, and effective coaching, when done well, are motivators to leaders and followers alike. Hence this section starts with reminding you how each of the previous sections serve as motivators. These final chapters offer a theory to help leaders inspire a motivated organization.

As I have articulated, my values are derived from the fact that I can make a difference in the world I live and, more importantly, make a difference in the world of the future. Consider your life's purpose. Mine is to help others understand their great potential in the hope they will do the same for others. I hope, through reading this book, you have been able to reflect on your life and your purpose. In realizing this purpose, I behave according to a set of basic values: Christ-centered, respect for the individual, responsible citizenship, integrity, and teamwork. Likewise, I hope you have discovered your values that define how you make decisions and behave. I am motivated to realize this purpose, and I am motivated to be recognized for living by these values. So can you and those you lead. Everything we have studied in transformational leadership pertains to negotiating constant change through constant learning. Learning is motivating. Coaching involves the leader in this learning and impacts the effort of the follower. Effort can be inspired through effective coaching; thus good coaching is motivating.

35. You Are a
Motivator Already

A Unifying Purpose Motivates

Goals that help an organization realize a selfless purpose that unifies efforts are inspirational and motivating when achieved. What makes the goal special is that it inspires achievement. It is motivating to accomplish goals that contribute to an organization realizing its selfless purpose. It is even more motivating when these accomplishments contribute to the discovered and realization of an individual's life purpose. How unifying and inspiring it is when each individual member of the team has discovered their personal purpose and understands they will move towards realizing that purpose as the organization realizes its purpose. They will have an inspired heart, and they will be motivated.

Remember August Turak's book, *The Business Practices of the Turkish Monks,* referred to in Chapter 6? The monk's purpose was driven by service and selflessness. The successful egg business was only a tool for the monks to realize their purpose. When the egg business was discontinued, another business was established as the tool to realize their purpose. The monks were inspired not by what they could get from the business but by what the business could give to making a better community—and that gift to the community had nothing to do with money. Each monk would be realizing his personal purpose if the monastery realized its purpose and they were motivated.

Similarly, Merck's mission of ridding the world of disease inspired employees to adopt personal purposes aligned with the organization's purpose and hearts were inspired.

Even my struggling health club mentioned in the book's introduction became an inspiration to staff and members when we established a purpose of helping those that were disenfranchised and, in our small way, participated in finding a cure for cancer. When an organization has a wholesome purpose that is, even in part, aligned with the personal purpose of everyone, you will have a motivated group of people inspired from the heart.

Values—Leaders with Values Inspire the Heart

Leaders who make decisions and behave according to a set of values inspire the hearts of those they lead. Their mere presence motivates those around them. Remember Rob in Chapter 11? He had a value that included serving others. When I was going through that difficult time after my wife died, he gave me a great idea, coached me on its execution, and then stepped back, allowing me to take the credit. He publicly recognized me for this success. My heart was inspired, and I was motivated.

Consider the wealth management example where efforts in one company were to motivate through cognitive rewards. Trips, bonuses, and publicly recognizing those who executed the most financial plans were countered by threats and coercive measure to those who did not support the strategy. These rewards were motivational, and I believe are important; however, when you compare those rewards to rewards recognizing the education and learning that selflessly focuses on bettering the position of the client, these results are not only longer lasting but help form a culture that is positive and motivating. Recognition that recognizes alignment within the organization's values has longer term positive impact in comparison to the more 'transactional' shorter term recognition. Longer-term goals that focus on values motivate the heart.

Recently my grandchildren were visiting. With the help of their father, they spent hours building a fort in the woods. They live a day's drive from me, and they were leaving the next morning. Why did they make such an effort building something that they would not be able to play in and enjoy? They were very motivated to complete this project. The motivation had to be derived from actually *building* the fort rather than playing in it.

So, it is with so many things, like financial planning. The inspiration of the heart does not come from seeing how many plans we could execute or even how much money we can make, rather, it comes through helping people make informed decisions that will impact their futures. For my grandchildren, the motivation resided in the process, the building, in creating something of value. Values came into play in both examples—the father was motivated to spend time with his children influencing them (a value of developing your children to be better citizens); the financial professional was motivated to serve clients (a value of putting the best interest of the client first).

As you lead your team, think of an example where you are trying to inspire others to accomplish something and through this effort you further embed a value that, in part, defines your organization or team.

I asked Donna, the CEO of the local nonprofit mentioned in Chapter 23, how she embedded values into her organization and how values can be a motivating force. She said she seldom sends an email or opens a meeting without referring to one of the organization's values and how a person or group made a decision or took an action that was inspired by supporting the value. It is motivating to have recognition like this from a supervisor. It is also motivating to get similar recognition from a peer or even a follower that highlights a selfless effort in support of wholesome values.

Imagine the pride you might feel when you are affirmed for living by a set of values that define you and your team. The pride in 'walking the walk' and being recognized for that journey is motivating.

For example, not too long ago in the local nonprofit just mentioned, a caregiver was changing a diaper of a six-month-old and forgot to spray the table down before starting (one of the 11 required steps to changing a diaper). The organization's definition of integrity is, "if you see an unsafe act that could jeopardize a child, you must take action." Admittedly, this is a unique definition. Another caregiver stepped up to correct the situation. Rather than being offended at being corrected, which was normal prior to this organization embedding values into the culture, she responded with "thank you," and both were inspired and proud of having a team that helps each other support the organization's values.

The unity that is inspired by a wholesome set of values that guides decisions and behaviors is directly connected to a highly motivated and cohesive team. Teams like this have inspired hearts and are motivated, making that motivation contagious.

Transformation — Learning, Changing, and Transforming Inspires the Heart.

Being in a transformational culture can be, in itself, motivating. Transformational leaders inspire learning, include followers in identifying needed change, build the capacity of the individual, and endear a transparent environment. In short, if you are a transformational leader, you are motivating your constituents.

In Chapter 24, I shared how my fifth-grade teacher, Mrs. Carney, inspired me to believe in myself. She replaced the judgmentalism of my fourth-grade teacher, Mrs. Schultz, with the positive approach needed to build my capacity to believe in myself: that I was valuable. It motivated me.

How motivating it is to be a part of the local 911 communications center highlighted in Chapter 25! Unlike just a few short years ago, today people take responsibility to be a learner. Mistakes are taken as opportunities to learn. People are allowed to be vulnerable as long as they learn from the risk. It is motivating to learn through dialogue that includes treating everyone in the conversation with equal value, knowing that the team wins rather than any one individual.

Even resolving conflict is motivating. I cannot forget Isadore Sharp described in Chapter 25, the founder of the Best Western Resorts, who resolved conflict by inspiring a dialogue between the disagreeing parties. Out of the dialogue emerged The Best Western Resorts worldwide. The emotion that accompanies conflict was soon stripped away and replaced by a motivated desire to find solutions together rather than finding lesser solutions as individuals. It is motivating to be a part of a transforming team that is in constant dialogue.

These types of environments make transparency a natural

part of the motivated transformational culture. Remember Liz in Chapter 26, who was afraid to constructively contribute to the groups dialogue? After the walls of insecurity were torn down, Liz, with courage, contributed immeasurably to the solution. It was motivating to Liz, certainly, but it was also motivating to all of us as a team.

Coaching—Great Coaches Inspire the Heart

Great coaches are great motivators. Embedded in the Supernova plan discussed in the coaching section of this book are goals and expectations (remember the *ruler* that specifically measures progress). These goals and outcomes bring clarity to expectations and give opportunity to celebrate achievement, which can be very motivational. This sort of recognition inspires a desire to perform at the exceptional level. The recognition of such performance is motivating.

These goals and outcomes can be tactical (such as revenue or sales numbers), be purpose-based in recognizing outcomes that help the organization realize its purpose or be values-driven in recognizing behaviors or decisions that conform to the organization's values. My point is that this inspiration is underwritten by great coaching. In the absence of coaching, great opportunities are lost with negative consequences. Let's take for example "The Cage."

Most brokerage offices, big and small, used to have wire operators that are responsible for sending and receiving secure information. Due to sensitive information being exchanged, these operators were located in an area that has controlled and limited access. The brokerage industry sometimes called this room "the cage," because it was often enclosed by a wire type wall so that it was easy to communicate to someone outside the room, yet access could still be controlled. I know, calling it "the cage" is not very motivating. I eventually asked people to refer to it as "the wire room" but that is another story.

Around Christmas time and the end of the year, it was my practice to hand out bonuses based on compensation and performance. The higher the compensation and the better the performance, the higher the bonus. On this particular day, just prior to Christmas, I walked around handing out bonus checks to the very deserving staff. I walked into the wire room to give the wire operator, Cathy, her bonus. Cathy had an annual base compensation package of about $40,000 and had been working with the company for about five years. I was smiling as I handed her a bonus check of $3,000. I told her she was doing a great job as I handed her the check. She smiled and thanked me.

As I walked out the door and was perceived to be out of hearing range (remember the walls were made of wire so one could easily communicate through them) I heard Cathy say, "I would gladly give up this money if John, or someone, would come in here once in a while and tell me I was doing a good job." This was over fifteen years ago, and her words still cut through me like a knife.

Though I was not Cathy's direct supervisor or coach (that responsibility was for the operations manager) I felt responsible for every employee's development and morale. This caused me to reflect on how well people were being coached and, through that coaching, how motivated they became. Were we really recognizing people for substantial accomplishment and progress, and were the accomplishments and progress a result of a good coaching process? Was the "Supernova" coaching process, described in Section 4, really being honored? As their coach, I have intimate knowledge of their failures and successes. The failures were celebrated through learning opportunities. The successes were celebrated, sometimes publicly and sometimes privately, to encourage good performance. The recognition was to authentically give credit for things that matter in a timely manner. The coaching relationship makes these celebrations authentic and is motivating.

As for Cathy, her boss, the operations manager, reported to me, and I began coaching her like I wanted Cathy to be coached (Section 4). The operations manager began modeling my coaching and efforts to celebrate achievements. Yet I still needed to recognize Cathy and others more. Much of her recognition and motivation would come from the Supernova coaching process. Her coach was pivotal in her development and her motivation.

But Cathy's story is not finished.

36. To Motivate Is to Know What Is Important

Recognizing constituents for contributing towards an organization's purpose while abiding by its values is important. However, to authentically motivate someone demands us to know what is important to that person. Take Cathy for instance and my oversight in properly recognizing her great performance. The following Sunday, following the bonus check day, I was standing on the balcony of my apartment overlooking Lake Eola in downtown Orlando. Around this beautiful inland lake was a popular asphalt walking path. On this perfect Sunday afternoon, I saw Cathy walking with her husband and two small children. The kids were running and playing as Cathy and her husband were holding hands as they walked and talked. The love contained in this family was apparent. I could not help but ask myself what it was like for her to go home every night trying to be a good wife and mother without getting recognition from her boss day in and day out.

Just by my saying, "Great Job, Cathy," perhaps her whole evening would be positively influenced, setting a positive tone for the entire family. How motivating it could have been for her and, in turn, for her family! Certainly, family was extremely important.

That moment reminded me that leaders have great power to impact not only individuals but also important things such as family. Just taking the opportunity to say "good job" when warranted and notice individuals for great performance can make a difference. Money was not the motivator for Cathy; genuine and authentic recognition from her boss was. For me to understand how important her family was to her was a critical ingredient to me being a motivator to Cathy.

Take the three brick layers I mentioned in Chapter 5. Remember, when asked, "What are you doing?" the first brick layer said, "Building a wall." The second said, "Building a church." The third replied, "Building the house of God." All three doing the same thing but motivated by very different reasons. Leaders need to know the reasons.

Most of us have seen the movie, *Jerry Maguire*. Rod Tidwell, played by Cuba Gooding Jr., is graduating from the University of Arizona as a star football player. Jerry Maguire, played by Tom Cruise, is hired by Tidwell to be his agent. If you have seen the movie, you certainly remember the "Show Me the Money" scene. Tidwell directs Maguire; if Maguire is to continue as his agent, to yell with meaning and force, "Show me the money!" Here Tidwell is trying to emphasize the importance of a big monetary contract to him and his family. One would naturally assume that money is a significant motivator for Tidwell (which I am sure it was). However, later in the movie, after he is drafted and given a sizeable contract, he catches a critical touchdown pass against the Dallas Cowboys, but after a hard hit is lying motionless in the end zone. The crowd is silent, and players from both teams' crowd around, obviously concerned about Tidwell's condition.

As Tidwell is revived by the staff who begin to help him up, he stops them. As he is lying there, he smiles and says, "Wait a minute. Let me enjoy this." All of a sudden Tidwell leaps up and does flips, jumps into the crowd, dances, and spins the football. The crowd responds with thunderous ovation, cheering Tidwell's touchdown and his apparent recovery from a vicious hit. Initially motivated by money, Tidwell's agent represents him very well and garners him a large contract to be sure. However, once the security the money brings his family is realized, what really motivates Tidwell is recognition.

Now ask yourself again (remember Chapter 4)… what are the five most important things in your life? Reflect on your answers. Now ask those that report to you the most important things in their lives. These things should be revealed in the coaching process. Write them down so you can always be reminded what is important to this individual. This is key knowledge to motivating the individuals that report to you.

37. Motivational Theory

What is your theory on motivation? Thus far I have argued that inspiring a wholesome purpose, guided by a set of values, which guides decisions and behaviors, can be motivating. Being in an environment that encourages education and personal development can inspire the heart. Also, having a good coach that focuses totally on the betterment of the one being coached can motivate.

But there is more. It would seem that a leader should have their own theory on what incentives are most effective to motivate followers. This chapter is intended to help you develop your own theory on incentives.

Incentive Theory

Most leaders have practiced what is known as the Incentive Theory. If you need to move your organization towards accomplishing shorter-term goals, it is logical to provide tangible incentives known to some as extrinsic (as opposed to intrinsic) motivations. If a tactical plan's outcome is to open up more accounts, attract more assets under management, to complete more financial plans, hire more people, get high marks on evaluations or tests, win awards, win contests, or make more money, and the short-term goals are achieved, then the Incentive Theory can be relevant. I have applied this theory both successfully and, unfortunately, unsuccessfully.

Where the achievement of such goals is extrinsic, my focus is on the reward or what I can get as opposed to a more selfless or wholesome intent. An example would be a student prioritizing a passing grade over expanding a knowledge base and learning. Or a corporate executive emphasizing a larger bonus over realizing a wholesome purpose. My experience indicates intrinsic motivation and internalization results in higher achievement; whereas, paradoxically, attempting to control achievement outcomes directly through extrinsic rewards leads to lower-quality motivation and performance.

I have been personally intoxicated with being recognized as a winner and rewarded with beautiful vacations. This theory can be effective when trying to achieve a performance that can be easily measured and reasonably handled over a short term. Where problems can arrive is when the recognition and the tangible prize receive more importance than they deserve.

The pressing question evolves around intent. Why do you want to win, or why are you extending such effort to accomplishing a goal? Is it because of what you can get (transactional), or is it because of the good you will do for others (transformational)? It is probably both, but the answer is personal and important.

The Incentive Theory has a danger of having too much focus on creating a culture that is self-serving (what I can get) rather than leading to more selfless motives (what I can give). It can be shortsighted.

In other words, if I have a contest that is intended to motivate certain behaviors and the contest is now concluded, what motivates me now? Or when I receive a bonus for achieving certain goals, do I then transition my efforts towards the goals for the next bonus? What motivates me if there is no bonus available? Do I just wait around for the next contest or bonus to see what I can win; or do I continue to behave and accomplish goals with the intent of doing good? Are my decisions and behaviors focused on a tangible incentive or focused on realizing the organization's purpose?

Hence, can motivating with incentives adversely affect a culture driven by purpose and values? Possibly, if the incentives receive more attention and degree of importance than they deserve.

When assessing the accuracy of a theory, it is important to identify its flaws or where the theory does not seem to apply. The Incentive Theory assumes that all people are motivated by money or some other tangible reward. I know some very hard-working people in the non-profit world that are not motivated by these tangible awards. They are motivated by how many children go on to college, how their efforts may have lowered the level of teenage pregnancies, or how their efforts contributed to a disabled person living a life of independence.

How does a pastor measure his success—by how much money he makes? I think not. Or how about some of my great classmates from West Point who stayed in the Army for an entire career? Those brilliant people could have left the service for more money, but many did not. Service to country was more important. The traditional Incentive Theory does not seem to apply in these cases. So, what theory may apply?

Hygiene Versus Motivational Factors

True motivation comes from getting people to do things because they want to do it. Realizing a wholesome purpose, making decisions, and behaving according to a set of values, learning, and transforming, or seeing the results of selfless coaching can be very motivating. But there is more. True motivation comes during both good and difficult times. Motivation also moves along a spectrum of environments that are highly motivating and happy on one end and miserable on the other. Is it possible to have a motivational theory that applies to the entire spectrum of environments? I think so.

Frederick Herzberg published an article in the *Harvard Business Review* that focuses on exactly this. His position was that satisfaction and dissatisfaction are separate entities and can be measured separately. I would add that they must also be studied and applied together for one set of measurement impacts the other. This theory distinguishes between two different types of factors: hygiene factors and motivational factors.

Hygiene factors are things like compensation, job security, work conditions, policies, or supervisory practices. If you feel underpaid, or you have a manager who does not respect you, you will be dissatisfied. When these situations are remedied, you become less dissatisfied—but not necessarily motivated. If hygiene factors are satisfied, that does not mean you will love your job. It will probably mean you will hate it less. Remedying hygiene factors will likely not satisfy you, but you become less dissatisfied. If you have an attrition problem in a workplace, look first at the hygiene factors that are disrupting motivated employees. Then fix the problems.

To bring this to life, let's consider Joe. Joe was a very good resident manager who ran an office of thirty employees. This operation generated about seventeen million dollars in revenue and was associated with a large, well-branded, brokerage company. Joe's compensation was based primarily on personal production as a financial advisor and, to a lesser degree, his role as a manager. Joe was about fifty years old and had several years as a financial advisor prior to taking the position as resident manager. His was a demanding and rewarding position that led him to be well respected in the community. He had everything to be a highly motivated professional, including great relationships with his advisors and with his immediate supervisor. He was respected and recognized for his maturity and problem solving.

The problem was compensation. Joe did not have enough income to support his standard of living. He felt he deserved higher compensation for his managerial responsibilities. But he was associated with a large firm that did not compensate this way. More compensation would depend upon him increasing his business as a financial advisor. But that takes time—time Joe was not willing to invest. So, he quit. His compensation, a hygiene factor, was not satisfactory to the level he wanted. The motivators like challenging work, recognition, the feeling of being valued and respected could not override Joe's dissatisfaction with his compensation.

It is important to address hygiene factors such as a safe and comfortable work environment, relationships with colleagues, and compensation. The consequences for inadequate hygiene factors will be a very dissatisfied employee, possibly an employee like Joe. However, satisfying hygiene factors alone will not cause your employees to love their job, rather it will prevent dissatisfaction.

Let's now consider motivational factors. Herzberg defines *motivators* as things that truly motivate. Challenging work, good relationships with supervisors, and recognition, are all examples of motivators. These motivators inspire the heart of constituents and must be considered by leaders who wish to motivate their peers and followers. Aspiring toward a wholesome purpose, for example, is a motivator. My fitness center had a purpose of helping the disenfranchised, and that was motivating to the employees. The soldier has a motivation to protect his country from enemies, foreign and domestic.

However, both the soldier and the employee need compensation that allows them to achieve an acceptable standard of living. The balance of motivators and hygiene factors is serious for leaders to consider for themselves and their constituents.

This is especially important to consider as leaders, but also play a role in personnel decision making as well. For example, I have seen disastrous consequences when only compensation, a hygiene factor, is considered in career decisions. In the picture of my West Point classmates, Scott was the best athlete and a tremendous swimmer. He was commissioned in the Army as a second lieutenant with great promise. After five years, he decided he had enough of the Army and opted to leave for higher compensation. A side effect of this decision was that he stopped his conditioning routine, which was no longer necessary in his new job. He focused his time and energy on making more money. It was not long before Scott died of complications associated with bad health choices. Again, too much emphasis on hygiene factors can bring disastrous results.

What about motivators? Are they any different if over-emphasized? Linda was a highly compensated executive who was let go from her position. She had plenty of money to live the rest of her life comfortably, but her position was her "branding." It was her motivator. Without the position, she spiraled into bad health habits, drinking too much, and not taking physical care of herself. Before long, she also passed away, leaving a son and husband behind. When your corporate or institutional position, a motivating factor, becomes the overriding focus of life, disastrous consequences can be the result. Too much emphasis on motivators, just like hygiene factors, can also bring disastrous results.

In review, both hygiene factors and motivators must be constantly monitored and kept in some degree of balance. Problems occur for leaders and for individuals when either one becomes a significant priority over the other. If hygiene factors are a problem, they must be fixed. If motivators are such a priority that hygiene factors are overlooked, then problems can occur without you knowing you have a problem. Leaders that motivate others will pay attention to both.

38. Concluding Thoughts and Action Steps on Motivating

This fifth and final section is crucial and my decision to make it the final section was quite intentional. It summarizes what had been emphasized in the preceding four sections. That review coupled with your development of your own motivational theory will inspire a motivated team led by you. Your theory should take into account the first four sections, but also appreciate how hygiene and motivational factors and incentives inspire the hearts and motivate your followers. The "Action Steps" should help you develop your own motivational theory.

Action Steps

1. Write down your life's purpose. Maybe review steps 1 thru 4 from Action Steps in section 1. Now conduct an inventory as to what you have done in the last week to contribute to realizing this purpose.

2. Consider an organization you are associated with (job, church, club, school, etc.). Write down their purpose and vision. Look it up if you cannot remember. How does

that organization in realizing its purpose help you realize your purpose?

3. What motivates you (money, recognition, security, family accomplishment, personal achievement)? Then write down (again) the five most important things in your life. Categorize each by hygiene factor or motivator factor.
4. What are you going to do to solve challenges with hygiene factors in the short term?
5. What are you going to do to instill motivator solutions in your life?
6. Go through steps 1 through 5 with everyone who reports to you. What are their hygiene factors and motivators? Develop a plan for each. Include knowledge on their values and purpose, what they need to learn to succeed in the future, and an organized and regimented coaching program for each.
7. What incentives motivate you?
8. What incentives motivate those that report to you?
9. Develop an incentive plan that addresses short-term goals and longer-term strategies that honor purpose and values.
10. What is your theory on motivation?

Contributing Work
to Section 5

These Works Helped Inspire
Some of the Key Concepts

Christenensen, C. M. (2012). *How Will You Measure Your Life.* London, Harper Collins.

Wiseman, L. (210). *Multipliers: How the Best Leaders Make Everyone Smarter.* New York, NY, HarperCollins Publishers.

Martin and Roger (2009). "The Opposable Mind: Winning Through Integrative Thinking." Boston, *Harvard Business Review.*

Kouzes, J. M. and B. Z. Posner (1995). *The Leadership Challenge: How to Get Extraordinary Things Done in Organizations.* San Francisco, CA, Jossey-Bass Publishers.

Bergman, P. (2018). *Leading with Emotional Courage.* Hoboken, NJ, John Wiley and Sons, Inc.

Turak, A. (2012). *The Trappist Way: Business Wisdom of the Trappist Monk*. Columbia, SC, Columbia University: 318.

Conclusion

Negotiating Turbulence was intended for leaders with some experiences and thus some personal stories that hopefully resonated with the stories in the book. My hope is that the book inspired you to go on a personal journey. To reflect on people you respected, and some you did not. That reflection may help you discover things that you did well and some things that could have been done better. That learning will be valuable in constructing a more effective leadership future.

Your personal journey in Section One helped you confirm or discover an overarching personal purpose that directs your path towards its realization. In Section Two we learned our path is framed by the values that define how you behave and make decisions. It keeps you centered on what is right—what you believe in. It is the key ingredient to what makes you the trusted leader. It is purpose and values that allow you to successfully negotiate the turbulence that is certain in leadership and in life.

The base of having beliefs formed from having purpose and values informs the great potential contained in the transformational leader, the leader coach, and the motivator. This concept allows the leader to form a leadership plan that is far from arbitrary, but very intentional.

A leadership development plan may include other dynamics not included in this book. However I am certain any plan must start with the theories presented here. I heartily suggest you ask every member of your leadership team to read *Negotiating Turbulence* and then follow the outlines, as a workshop, by assembling your teams quarterly to go through each section one at a time. That effort will be the best team building exercise you could ever do and you will embed a culture in your organization that is intentional, positive, and strong.

Good luck in applying the principals presented in this book. The health of our communities rests with leaders like you who can successfully negotiate the turbulence of our times.

Acknowledgements

This book is built on stories that were made possible by their participants. I am grateful to you. In particular those leaders that were part of a 'good' story and thus represented themselves as the respected, or selfless, leader. Thank you for your example. I owe gratitude to my principal editor, Pattie Parker. Thank you, Pattie, for your conscientious efforts to bring these stories to life. To my great friend Neil Begley who was the first person I met at West Point and was also the first to represent a set of values that I would later model in life. Thank you old friend and rest in peace. To my daughters Angela and Katie who have taught me so many life lessons. You have been my inspiration that has caused me never to lose hope and to always believe that, no matter what, He loves us and will never give up on us. You are my heroes. To my grandchildren Jacob, Anna, John, Elijah, Titus, and Kilton. I love you more than you know. The biggest motivation I had for writing this book was knowing that someday you would read it. And finally to my wife Trish, the greatest treasure in my life. Your selflessness should serve as an example to all leaders. You do things for others in ways that nobody knows but you and the Creator. I love you and am so lucky to have you as my life partner. Lastly, you, the reader. Thank you for reading my book. Please take the theories to heart and become the respected leader of the future. You can change the world for the better. Believe it.

About the Author

Dr. Cosgrove is the founder and CEO of The Leadership Work-shop, LLC, owns a financial business, and is philanthropically in-volved in his church and the local nonprofit community. He is the father of two daughters and the grandfather of 6 grandchildren. He currently lives in Ooltewah, Tennessee with his wife Trish.

Dr. Cosgrove attended the United States Military Academy at West Point and earned a commission as an officer in the United States Army. While in the service he commanded a company in the Presidential Honor Guard, distinguished himself as an Airborne Ranger Infantry officer, and earned a Master of Science from the University of Wisconsin. He further distinguished himself as the distinguished honor graduate of the United States Army Ranger School of which has been argued as the most difficult school in the Armed Forces.

Upon leaving the service Dr. Cosgrove entered the business sector as a financial advisor with Merrill Lynch. He was eventually appointed as a director and managed a large region in the central part of the country. Twice Dr. Cosgrove was recognized as the best manager in the Merrill Lynch system. Upon leaving Merrill Lynch he became the President of Mellon Bank Financial Advisors followed by being appointed as a Senior Vice President for UBS.

Upon leaving the corporate sector Dr. Cosgrove founded several businesses to include the Leadership Workshop, LLC. He enrolled at Andrews University and earned a PhD in Leadership and wrote and published articles on leadership. Today Dr. Cosgrove travels all over the world talking on leadership and moderating leadership workshop with the hope of improving leadership in our communities.